COLOR FOR INTERIOR DESIGN

Ethel Rompilla
New York School of Interior Design

color

FOR INTERIOR DESIGN

Harry N. Abrams, Inc., Publishers

Library of Congress Cataloging-in-Publication Data

Rompilla, Ethel.
    Color for interior design / Ethel Rompilla
    and the New York School of Interior Design.
          p.   cm.
    Includes bibliographical references and index.
    ISBN 0–8109–5888–0 (alk. paper)
    1. Color in interior decoration. I. New York
    School of Interior Design. II. Title.

NK2115.5.C6R66 2005
747'.94—DC22
2004021040

Published in 2005 by Harry N. Abrams,
Incorporated, New York.

Printed and bound in China

10 9 8 7 6 5 4 3 2 1

Harry N. Abrams, Inc.
100 Fifth Avenue
New York, N.Y. 10011
www.abramsbooks.com

Abrams is subsidiary of

Editorial Concept Development
Richard Olsen
Editor, New York School of Design
Susan Lovell
Editor, Harry N. Abrams
Elaine M. Stainton
Photo Editor
Leslie Dutcher
Design
HvAD [Henk van Assen, Amanda Bowers
and Sarah Gifford]
Production Manager
Justine Keefe

New York School of Interior Design is chartered by
the Board of Regents of the University of the State of
New York and is an accredited institutional member
of the National Association of Schools of Art and
Design (NASAD). Its BFA program is accredited by the
Foundation for Interior Design Research (FIDER).

Ethel Rompilla received her bachelor of fine arts
degree in interior design from the New York School
of Interior Design and has taught color theory at
the college for the last 17 years. She has served as an
academic advisor and associate dean of the School
and remains a member of its faculty. In 1997 she was
the recipient of the William Breger Faculty Achieve-
ment Award. Her work experience includes high-end
residential design as well as commercial work for one
of the country's leading architectural firms. She is
an allied member of the American Society of Interior
Designers (ASID), a member of The Decorators Club,
and was involved in the preparation of first edition
of The New Munsell Student Color Set.

Front cover: A room by Debra Blair (see p. 172).
Back cover: A contemporary bedroom by Holger Schubert (see p. 206).
Frontispiece: Detail of *Suprematist Painting,* 1915, by Kasimir Malevich (p. 158).
Page 6: Detail of *Edward I of England Kneeling in Homage before Philippe le Bel of France,* c. 1460 (p. 69).

This book would not be possible without the help of the following individuals, to whom I am very grateful: first of all, to Inge Heckel, President of the New York School of Interior Design (NYSID), for her continuing encouragement and support in making this book possible. Special thanks also go to Susan Lovell, Director of Publications at NYSID, whose skillful editing turned my rough draft into a coherent and readable form, and who took on the added responsibility of acting as the book's photo editor.

My thanks go to others at NYSID: fellow color instructor Addie Sels, for her insight and helpful comments; Paul Glassman and Christopher Spinelli, for their help with library resources; Thomas Sowinski and Jason Lang, for computer counseling; to students Tom Tredway, for researching trends from the 1950s through the 1970s; Jared Jacobson, for computerized drawings; George Marshall Peters, for the freehand sketches; and to all students present and past for their enthusiasm and interest in color.

I would also like to acknowledge the dedicated faculty members who, over the years, developed a practical color course for interior designers that combines theory and creativity. These go back to the earliest years of the school, to the late Lucy B. Taylor, who studied under Albert Munsell.

On the publisher's side, I would like to thank the late Paul Gottlieb, Editor in Chief at Harry N. Abrams, Inc., and senior editor Richard Olson, who seized on the idea of a book and moved it along; senior editor Elaine Stainton, for her knowledge and expert polishing of words and phrases; designer Henk van Assen, for combining words and pictures with creative elegance; Leslie Dutcher, for taking on the endless task of photo research; production manager Justine Keefe, for overseeing the printing and color correction; and all others who worked quietly behind the scenes.

ACKNOWLEDGMENTS

MANY YEARS AGO MY PROFESSOR in a course on the history of architecture often repeated the phrase "architecture parle," or "architecture speaks." He urged us to look at a building not merely in descriptive terms, but in analytical terms as well, to delve into its underlying concept and the message it conveyed. Years of museum visits have taught me that color speaks in paintings, too. It also whispers, sings, and shouts. These experiences have provided the foundation for my observation of color in interior design.

Interior design requires both creative and technical skills, and a strong foundation in the history of the fine and decorative arts, interiors, architecture, and furniture. A common element can be found in the use of color, which is inseparable from good design. There are those who have a highly developed sense of color; others may have this talent to a lesser degree, or be comfortable working only with colors they like.

Too often color selection for interiors is approached in a casual way, as one would choose a necktie or lipstick. Selections are made, and color becomes an afterthought, even though it represents a larger and more permanent investment than any fashion choice. A designer must move beyond personal color preferences and speculative choices to make sound decisions for the clients they serve. Intuition and creativity do not have to be abandoned; instincts are good and should be heeded, but the skilled professional must be able to step back and understand the reason behind these feelings. Well-planned, logical choices are apt to produce a successful outcome and eliminate costly mistakes.

In order to help make these decisions, a designer needs a basic, broad range of knowledge in the history, theory, psychology, and philosophy of color, as well as good instincts. This book is not meant to be an authoritative guide; its purpose is to create an awareness of the many facets of this engaging topic. There are numerous studies by prominent theorists and outstanding texts on color; some are recent, others go back in time. It is hoped that this introduction will persuade the reader of the need for further exploration of these references and as well as continuing study. The intent is not to promote any one style or period over another, or color versus non-color, but to show how decorative styles and attitudes toward color change over time. History has a way of resurrecting itself in newly creative ways.

The study of color can be approached in a way similar to that of an appraiser who compares an antique piece of furniture with a reproduction, or an original work of fine art with a copy. The aim is to become sensitized to the very fine nuances of color through study, hands-on practice, analysis and evaluation, exchange of ideas with others, and the guidance of professionals. Human choices are highly individual. There

INTRODUCTION

may be a fear of commitment to color and uncertainty as to its proper use. And every decade has its popular trends, from avocado green and harvest gold to plum and teal blue, which invade every corner of the market from fashion to home furnishings, and in due time disappear into history. Some are lasting, others faddish and short-lived. Many are predicated by architectural trends, such as the transparency of modern buildings. In the last few decades, beige and white have predominated, and it is difficult to find the once popular floral patterns. Neutrals are ageless and work well with contemporary interiors, so this trend has endured. But change is a constant in life; people get bored with sameness, and what is discarded is inevitably resurrected in some form or other in the future. The perception of harmony may change, but color will always be in style.

Page 8: Detail of *Black Lines No. 189,* by Wassily Kandinsky (p. 154).
Opposite: The Schroeder House (pp. 152–53).

1

A
HISTORY
OF
COLOR

1

THE HISTORY OF COLOR IN INTERIORS is written on the walls of caves and tombs, cathedrals, palaces, and ordinary homes. From the time our prehistoric ancestors sought shelter from the elements, they brought nature inside. They used fire as a source of light, and then, using earth pigments, produced extraordinary paintings of animals on the walls of their caves. Later civilizations continued this tradition of bringing naturalistic forms indoors, both spiritual—as in the hieroglyphics of Egyptian tombs or carved foliage in Gothic cathedrals—and temporal, in the form of the floral tapestries, carpets, and paintings that graced castle and palace walls.

Some of the first-known pigments were harvested from the earth more than 30,000 years ago to produce thousands of realistic and spirited images of animals on the walls and ceilings of caves. Drawings of horses and bison captured the energy of these creatures in simple earth tones of red and yellow ocher and black. These earliest drawings are a reminder of the extraordinary creativity exhibited by prehistoric civilizations and how this force has continued through the arts of succeeding generations. The artist did not have the tools to sketch on site, and therefore an image of animals in motion had to be captured in the mind and later painted.[1] Anyone who has tried to draw a still object from memory, let alone a moving one, can fully understand the challenge.

From ancient Egypt, one of the most documented civilizations, well-preserved wall and ceiling paintings, as well as carvings in temples and tombs provide a visual narrative ranging from the tranquil activities of daily life to expeditions, battle scenes, and guides to the hereafter. Earth pigments continued to be in use—red and yellow ocher, along with blue, green, purple, black, white, and gray. A formula was applied to color: red ocher was used for the skin color of Egyptian men; yellow for the women; and brown for Nubians; pale bluish gray, white, or yellow provided background color; and black was used for hair and outlines. Blue was used for the sky and river, and purple for earth. Green depicted the fertile strip along the Nile and was also assigned to the god of resurrection, Osiris, sometimes portrayed wrapped in white mummy linens with a green face and hands. Although early tombs were simple, the burial chamber of Unas, last king of the fifth dynasty (2345 BC), reached elaborate proportions; the ceiling, painted dark blue with gold stars, brought the night sky inside—a theme to be repeated in later centuries.

The Palace of Knossos (c. 1700–1300 BC), ruins from the ancient Minoan civilization on the island of Crete, was, unlike the pyramids, a home for the living. Its most distinctive feature is the use of large red and black columns, tapered at the base, which resemble overturned tree trunks. Their strong colors emphasize their bulk. Standing

Prehistory to the Renaissance: Italy and Greece

walls of the palace are covered with frescoes; among them is the "Toreador" fresco, which may be related to the legend of Theseus, who was able to rescue his fellow Athenean youths from the half-bull, half-human minotaur. The most colorful frescoes are those in the so-called Throne Room, where bright red walls are divided by a wavy white horizontal band, an odd color combination that may represent clouds or water, or, in a more intriguing theory, the waves of earthquake activity common in the area.[2] Blue is prominent in the Queen's Megaron, a room in which painted dolphins swim gracefully along the upper wall over a border of stylized rosettes. Scenes of athletes in the Knossos frescoes foreshadow the athletic ideals of ancient Greece, where the symmetry and proportion of the human body carried over to sculpture as well as to the distinctive red and black pottery of the time. Beauty and harmony were ideals, and observation and logic prevailed. Mathematics and the principles of geometry provided the foundation for classical architecture, whose perfection of proportions in temples such as the Parthenon (447–38 BC) has never been surpassed. Decorative elements were considered to be subservient to structure, but in later centuries they would become the foundation for period design in interiors and furniture. One of the great controversies regarding ancient Greece was over whether the marble of Greek architecture was painted or not. The possibility that the pristine marble originally had been painted had been discussed but not widely accepted, until excavations in the nineteenth century confirmed that both the exterior and interior were indeed painted in vivid colors of red, yellow, blue, and green.

As power shifted to Rome, Greek architecture was adopted but modified. Marcus Vitruvius Pollio (first century BC), a Roman architect and engineer, established a module governing the dimensions and proportions of the orders of architecture. This also provided a template to carry the official style of building to the provinces and later became a guide for the revival of classical architecture in the Renaissance. Wealthy Romans had a fondness for nature and escaped to the country for relaxation and entertainment and, in some cases, to working farms. There was a shift to an awareness of the comfort of the individual and, with this, the emergence of interior decoration that we can relate to. Ruins of villas, covered by volcanic ash when Vesuvius erupted in AD 79, may be found in and around the cities of Pompeii and Herculaneum. Mid-eighteenth-century excavations uncovered some of the most colorful and remarkable examples of Roman art. Rooms in early villas were gathered around an interior courtyard, and panoramic scenes were brought indoors with frescoes that covered walls and ceilings.

In their buildings, the Romans made use of color both in natural materials such as marble and stone mosaic paving and in wall painting. Colors were brilliant in order to

1. Silvano Arieti, *Creativity,*
The Magic Synthesis, 194
2. Vincent Scully, *Architecture,*
The Natural and the Manmade, 35
Scully describes "…a deep ripple
like an earthquake tremor runs…"
behind the throne.

Page 14: Detail of *The Lady and the Unicorn* tapestry (p. 21).
Above: The Palace of Knossos. In the restored Throne Room, placid griffins and green foliage buffer fiery red walls.

be effective in the dim interior light: bright red, green, yellow, blue, and blue-green in a range of tonal values, in addition to ivory, brown, and black. Walls were given a polished finish, perhaps to resemble marble, reflect light, or protect the paint. Flooring made use of colored glass or marble as well, or mosaic floors in black and white provided a neutral background.

A villa at Boscotrecase, near Pompeii, had a black room, a bedroom overlooking the bay of Naples.[3] The black upper portion of the wall rests on a red dado, and the two colors are separated by thin horizontal bands of green and white. Red was symbolic of the sun or light, and black of darkness or night. The juxtaposition of colors might be interpreted as the sun rising, or darkness descending, over the horizon. While the red and black columns at Knossos felt heavy, the same colors used on the walls here are lightened by the painting of thin and delicate columns, figures, and borders. In a reversal of large outdoor scenes that cover walls in other Pompeian interiors, the black bedroom has, centered on the wall, a very small painting of a tower as it would be seen in the distance when framed by a window.

Centuries later, in medieval times, color was most commonly seen in religious art—illuminated manuscripts, altarpieces, and stained-glass windows in Gothic cathedrals, with the added drama of diffused light at different times of day. Warmth as well as color was added to fortresslike castle walls by large tapestries, which were intricately woven works with religious or allegorical themes. Nature was celebrated with scenes showing plants, trees, animals, and birds. The colors of these tapestries, now softened by time, still glow with red, yellow, light and dark blues and greens, brown, and off-whites.

In his book, *Color for Interiors, Historical and Modern*, color theorist Faber Birren (1900–88) states that prior to the Renaissance there was a "classical tradition" of color in which choices were determined by religion or myth, not by the individual; the basic palette of red, yellow, blue, green, and purple, plus black and white, depended on the materials available. The Renaissance brought freedom from past constraints in thought, and, with this, the "creative tradition" emerged: the artist's palette produced a wide range of values and chroma, and color became highly refined. The Renaissance, which by the fourteenth century began to emerge in Italy and which reached its peak in the fifteenth and sixteenth centuries, brought a return to classical principles and philosophy after the medieval period. Greek and Roman art and ideas were rediscovered, and, in addition to religious subjects, nonreligious themes could be explored in art and decoration.

Opposite: Jacques Ignace Hittorff, a prominent nineteenth-century French architect, was one of the leading figures in the study of the polychroming of ancient Greek temples. This illustration is from his *Restitution du temple d'Empèdocle à Sélinonte; ou L'Architecture polychrome chez les Grecs* (1851). The philosopher Empedocles (c. 495–35 BC), presaged modern physics in his teachings that the earth was composed of four elements: earth, air, fire, and water.

3. A major portion of this room is at The Metropolitan Museum of Art, New York City.

Above: A section of one wall in the black bedroom of a villa at Boscotrecase, which survived destruction by Mount Vesuvius. Spindly columns lighten the weight of heavy black walls, while a miniature landscape scene with a tower reflects an exterior view.

Opposite: A panel of *The Lady and the Unicorn* tapestries at the Cluny Museum, Paris. The forms and colors of nature were carried indoors in these woven paintings.

The Davanzati Palace, Florence. Geometry and color are used to
break down the massive scale of the third-floor bedroom walls in
this medieval palazzo.

The fourteenth-century Davanzati Palace in Florence is a textbook example of a palace in transition from a medieval to a Renaissance style. The tall Gothic fireplace and painted wooden ceiling beams remained, but the walls were divided into geometric segments decorated with pattern and color and crowned with a painted cornice of arches to mitigate the size of the large rooms. Vivid colors of earlier periods were retained, but were expanded in tonal and chromatic value to become more elaborate and refined. Virtually all surfaces were covered, and there was an extravagant use of gold. Colors were brilliant reds, medium to deep blues and greens, yellow ocher, browns, and off-white. Later in the Renaissance, these colors softened. Silks, damasks, velvets, and tapestries were used for drapery and wall coverings. Long before developing its own industries, Italy was an important trade link between Europe and the Byzantine Empire, which produced luxurious silks.

Pompeii was still buried under the ashes of Vesuvius, when, in the sixteenth century, the country villa again provided a retreat from the city. The architect Andrea Palladio (1508–1580) studied the works of Vitruvius and also measured ancient Roman ruins. Palladio interpreted the classic style in his own way in the villas he designed in the vicinity of Venice, combining beauty with function while paying heed to his clients' needs. Large rooms were balanced with smaller ones. Nature was brought inside in the form of trompe l'oeil frescoes, with their illusion of depth created by the contrast of light and shadow on pale backgrounds. *The Four Books of Architecture,* a collection of Palladio's drawings based on his studies, would become a standard reference for architects in centuries to come.

THE RENAISSANCE INFLUENCE SPREAD northward from Italy to France with Francis I (1494–1547), who admired Italian painters and invited artists, architects, and artisans to work in the construction and decoration of royal residences. Fontainebleau, near Paris, was turned into a stunning example of French Renaissance architecture, with significant interior innovations. For the first time, Italian artisans combined classic details of rectangular wood panel wainscoting with frescoes on the wall above in light colors and surrounded them with figures in high relief using stucco instead of stone. The darker wood paneling below seemed to lift the lighter frescoes above. The order was then reversed—the wainscot portion of the wall was painted a light gray as a backdrop for delicate panels of nature scenes and floral motifs, while the paintings on the upper wall were dark. This reversal introduced lighter walls, which would be a major influence in periods to come.[1]

Versailles began as a modest hunting lodge built by Louis XIII in 1623 in the countryside near Paris and was later enlarged to a small chateau. Some thirty-eight years later, Louis XIV, the Sun King, set plans in motion to make Versailles one of the most magnificent of royal residences. Architects, gardeners, and artists worked not to copy, but to interpret, the Italian style to develop one that was truly French. The status of the artist was elevated, academies for their training were opened, and students were sent to Italy to study.

By this time, Italian art had shifted to the baroque style, which embodied a new freedom of form and movement in painting, sculpture, and architecture. Classical order gave way to exuberant curves on a grand scale, and, as French artists returned home, they brought with them these new ideas, to architecture as well as decoration. The French government established workshops to manufacture a dazzling array of tapestries, porcelains, furniture, fabrics, carpets, and they uncovered the secret of Venetian glass-making.

The massive scale of the rooms at Versailles dictated bold colors, and no surface was left unadorned. Gobelins tapestries, silk damasks, and velvets—often with large and contrasting patterns and elaborate fringes and trims—in vibrant red, green, blue, and gold were used to cover furniture and walls. As the artist's palette developed into to a wider range of lights, darks, neutrals, and pastels in addition to vivid colors, these changes were seen in interiors as well. Oak wall paneling was painted off-white to create a neutral background and then was heavily gilded. Various woods were inlaid on cabinets, desks, and parquet floors. Marble was lavishly used on walls and floors, its variegated textures adding further exuberance. Mirrors reflected the light of monumental chandeliers.

The Sixteenth–Eighteenth Centuries in France, England, and America

Before the young Louis XV assumed the throne in 1723, work continued on the interior of Versailles during the Regency (1715–23). The baroque style evolved into the rococo, with its decorative shell motifs. Rigid formality was relaxed, and rooms became smaller and more comfortable. Arabesques, flowers, and leaves—colored or gilded—softened the wall panels. The centers of panels were often painted with chinoiserie or pastoral scenes as a less expensive option to carved decoration. Hand-painted wallpapers from China were also used. The paneling in some rooms was left in natural wood, but most often it was painted in neutral tints of green or blue or in creamy or cool whites and embellished with gilt. Although damask, velvet, tapestry, and brocade were used for upholstery, there was a trend toward lighter silks and the less expensive, hand-blocked cotton and linen toile manufactured in Jouy, near Versailles, and printed with pastoral scenes in blue, green, red, or purple on a natural cream background.

The colors of eighteenth-century textiles, carpets, and furniture have faded through the years, but the vibrancy of their colors can be seen in porcelains of the time. At the Sèvres porcelain factory—which was moved from Vincennes to be closer to Versailles at the encouragement of Mme. de Pompadour, the king's mistress and an avid collector—exquisitely detailed drawings were painted on ground colors of *vert pommes* (apple green), *bleu céleste* (turquoise), *bleu nouveau* (dark blue), *jaune* (yellow), and, of course, *rose pompadour.*

Even before Louis XVI ascended the throne in 1774, changes had begun around mid-century with the excavations at Pompeii and Herculaneum. Books and drawings recorded these discoveries, inspiring a return to symmetrical lines, mechanical curves, and discreet ornament to form a new neoclassical style. Wall paneling reverted to simple, rectangular shapes and was painted white or pale gray with a hint of color and added gilt. Panels were often inset with fabric or wallpaper, and moldings were painted a contrasting color or highlighted with a colored shadow line. Aubusson, Savonnerie, or oriental carpets were placed over parquet floors. Damasks, brocades, taffetas, needlepoint, tapestries, and printed cottons were used for furniture, draperies, and wall coverings. Patterns included delicate florals, stripes, ribbons, and Chinese motifs. Despite the significant shift in architecture and furniture, this revived "classical style" was not paired with the vivid colors of antiquity but rather, because of its smaller scale, with the "creative style" of the Renaissance in a softer palette of yellow-green, pink, beige, rose, light blue, and gold.[2]

The upheaval of the French revolution in 1789 limited changes in furniture and decoration. Several years later, the interim Directoire provided a transition between the straight simplicity of the Louis XVI style and the more robust, military empire style

1. *Connaissance des Arts, Fontaine-bleau, The Gallery of Francis I, The King's Cabinet,* 23–26
2. Faber Birren, *Color for Interiors, Historical and Modern,* 48

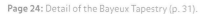

Page 24: Detail of the Bayeux Tapestry (p. 31).
Above: The Queen's Bedroom at Versailles restored to its appearance when occupied by Marie Antoinette. The delicacy of the floral silk brocade reflects the lighter, more varied color palette of the late eighteenth century.
Right: Sèvres porcelain vase, c. 1775, on turquoise blue ground with gold, shows a pastoral scene inspired by a Boucher engraving. *The Metropolitan Museum of Art*

of Napoleon. Interest in the classics remained strong, and artists were influential in promoting it. A painting in the Louvre by Jacques-Louis David in 1788, *The Love of Paris and Helen*, shows a Pompeian tripod table, based on Etruscan or early Roman forms, and Grecian architectural elements. When Napoleon Bonaparte became emperor in 1804, he promoted a style that would magnify his victories. The motifs of past civilizations—including hieroglyphics, sphinxes, griffins, classical arabesques, Greek vases, Roman lamps, and laurel wreaths—were used as decorative elements. Other favored symbols were the emperor's "N" monogram, and the bee. As patron of the now prosperous furniture industry, Napoleon refurnished his private apartments at Fontainebleau and Versailles in the deep rich colors of the Empire period—a brilliant yellowish green, sky blue, yellow, ruby red, gold, brown, and violet; these played in contrast against white, pale gray, or other neutrals.

England

While the Renaissance flourished in Italy and was taking root in France, England in 1500 was still in the Gothic period. The medieval castle gave way to a more open form of domestic architecture in the sixteenth century. The typical Tudor or Elizabethan hall—an all-purpose room for eating, sleeping, and entertainment—had a stone floor, beamed ceiling, and either whitewashed walls or wainscoting with white plaster above. Wainscoting evolved from simple vertical plank boards to plain rectangular panels to panels with a carved linen-fold pattern, and they were often painted in a favored color such as green.

In England too, nature was brought indoors. Arras tapestries from France or less expensive painted wall hangings gave color and warmth to walls. Development of the decorative arts was prompted by trade, first in Italian silks and glass and Turkish carpets, and later, with the founding of the East India Company in 1600, in trade with the Orient. The Coromandel Coast of India supplied palampores, the hand-painted cotton fabrics with a tree of life motif that evolved into floral chintz, one of the most popular textiles to this day.

Although English period styles are named after monarchs, the English courts, unlike those of France, were not the primary force in the setting of taste. The break with Rome by Henry VIII in the early sixteenth century kept contact with Italy minimal until the early eighteenth century, when the Grand Tour, a trip to study arts and architecture, became an important part of an English nobleman's education. Italy was the primary destination for these young scholars set on absorbing culture and acquiring a new level of taste, as well as countless books, paintings, and antiquities. An early patron of the

---

Opposite, above: The Crillon Room, 1777–80, Paris. The Metropolitan Museum of Art. Graceful arabesques with flowers and birds lighten the symmetry of the rectangular wall panels and furniture. Pale tinted walls and green silk upholstery provide a cool background for warmer woods in this neoclassical interior. The mechanical table is by Jean-Henri Riesener, a noted cabinetmaker of the period, and it was made in 1780–81 for Marie Antoinette's rooms at Versailles.

Opposite, below: After her divorce from Napoleon, the Empress Josephine retired to her home at Malmaison near Paris. Her bedroom, c. 1812, is decorated in bright red silk with gold embroidery. The military tent motif was popularized by architects Charles Percier and Pierre Fontaine, appointed by Napoleon to develop the new Empire Style. The swan and the rose were two of Josephine's favorite motifs; "Rose" was one of her given names, and its many varieties filled the gardens at Malmaison.

Left: Longthorpe Tower, Northamptonshire. The tower was added in the fourteenth century to a thirteenth-century hall. The didactic themes of stained glass windows in medieval cathedrals were brought into domestic architecture; here the opposing forces of the spiritual and earthly are depicted in murals painted in red ochers on the Great Chamber's walls. A giant figure is shown at the Wheel of the Five Senses. *(The English Country House Through Seven Centuries, 32–35)*

Above, right: Haddon Hall, Derbyshire, c.1500. As wall panels took on classic elements, they were at first awkwardly proportioned. An example of sixteenth-century transition from medieval to Renaissance paneling can be seen in the irregular rectangular panels of the dining room. Red and white squares and heraldic motifs cover the wood ceiling and beams. *The English Country House,* 38

Below, right: A structure added to the medieval great hall had an upper room or "solar" (meaning "sun"), which functioned as a private apartment. This portion of the Bayeux Tapestry shows the English King Harold and others in such a room accessed by a narrow exterior stair. *The English Country House,* 16

arts, the Earl of Arundel, took the young artist Inigo Jones to Italy in 1613 to study Roman ruins, Renaissance architecture, and the works of Andrea Palladio. Jones returned with a copy of *The Four Books of Architecture* and, in addition to bringing classicism to England, has been credited with separating the roles of architect and craftsman by having drawings dictate the result.

The most notable architect after Inigo Jones, and to some, one of the most important in the history of architecture, was Sir Christopher Wren. He admired the work of Palladio, but after a visit to France (1665–66), he developed an interest in the baroque style and the classical French tradition. His ability to combine these varied elements with elegance influenced the development in England and America of the Georgian style, named after kings George I, II, and III, who ruled during the eighteenth century.

When the English Renaissance was at its peak in the seventeenth century, colors were bright—reds, blues, green, and gold—in medium or dark values in silks, damasks, brocades, velvets, and leather seen against neutral walls. In the early eighteenth century, green emerged as a popular color of the Georgian period. The range of medium to dark values, from yellow- to blue-greens, became lighter later on, and the popularity of this color range was carried to America.

As in eighteenth-century France, a growing dissatisfaction in England with curved baroque and rococo forms and a renewed interest in antiquity prompted a shift to a neoclassical style that lasted until the early nineteenth century. In 1754, Robert Adam, son of a prominent Scottish architect, began a four-year tour of Italy to study and measure Roman ruins. He also traveled across the Adriatic Sea to the Dalmatian coast to study ruins of the palace (c. 300 AD) of the Roman emperor Diocletian at Spalato (present day Split, Croatia). On his return, he produced a folio of drawings of the Roman palace and other ruins, and the projects that followed were to have a lasting effect on English architecture and interior design.

Adam was also influenced on his travels by the newly discovered ruins at Pompeii, which were being excavated during his stay, as well as by Italian and French Renaissance architecture. Adam's interpretation of classical architecture in his own style is evident in his later work at Syon House and other interiors.

Robert Adam is known as much for his interiors and use of color as he is for his architecture. He controlled every surface and detail, designed furniture and carpets, and was innovative in his use of texture, pattern, and color. Delicate arabesques, scrolls, garlands, urns, and vases added texture to walls, ceilings, and furniture. Low-relief moldings were painted white to raise them higher visually and give them an illusion of more depth against a colored background. Instead of using the saturated colors of

Opposite: Queen's House, Greenwich, Inigo Jones, early seventeenth century. The classical clarity and simplicity of its exterior is carried into the two-story hall, which is capped with an Italianate plaster ceiling. In a departure from the Elizabethan great hall, which was a multi-purpose room for living, this hall functions as a passage, a room for movement and circulation.

Left: Roman influence can be seen in the black and white entrance hall at Syon, designed in 1762 by Robert Adam. In this transition from the exterior to interior, architecture and geometry take precedence over color. The long, rectangular proportions of the room are minimized by an apse with a coffered ceiling at the far end, and also by the pattern in the marble floor—a square set on the diagonal—which is repeated in the ceiling.

Above, left: The anteroom at Syon, adjacent to the black and white entrance hall, retains an architectural look with its marble columns topped by Ionic capitals, but color is now predominant in a varied range of greens, red, yellow, brown, and extensive gilding. The bold scagliola floor pattern is a dominant feature in the room.

Above, right: Engraving by Robert Adam of ruins of the palace of the emperor Diocletian at Spalato, 1764.

antiquity on his classic forms, he used a range of pale tints or pastel blues, yellow, pink, and green, or a stronger rose red, blue, green, and gold, balanced by off-whites, neutral grays, warm browns, and black.

In his remodeling of rooms at Syon House, Middlesex, in 1762, Adam orchestrated a progression of contrasts from little color to vivid color. The white and black entrance hall, in a transition from the exterior, has little furniture and is decorated with statuary instead of paintings. This pristine hall leads to an anteroom filled with architectural detail vibrant with extensive gilding, a boldly patterned scagliola (an imitation marble) floor in green, red, yellow, and brown, and green marble columns. The adjacent dining room reverts to the white of the entrance hall, and it has statuary set in niches. The next room, the Crimson Drawing Room, has bright red walls, and the ceiling paterae (an oval or round disk inset with ornament) recall those in the apse of the entry hall, although these are colored. In the next room, a long gallery, the colors fade off into quiet pastel pinks and greens.

America

While Inigo Jones was traveling to Italy in the early seventeenth century, settlers from England were descending on American soil to establish colonies in Jamestown, Virginia (1607), and Plymouth, Massachusetts (1620). As one of the immediate needs for survival was shelter, small and simple two-room homes were made of local wood in the traditional style of their homeland. The inside face of the exterior wall was plastered, while the remaining walls and floor were of random-width planks in oak or pine. Furniture was simple and utilitarian, and textiles that were not imported were either roughly woven or needlepoint. Colors depended entirely on materials at hand, and yellow ocher, red, and green were usually limited to textiles or painted designs on furniture.

The migration of settlers from other European countries created a hybrid of regional styles. With an increase in trade and commerce, colonists turned to Europe for culture and refinement, and the early part of the eighteenth century saw a degree of emerging luxury in American Georgian interiors. Using pattern books, cabinetmakers followed English styles. Walls and woodwork were painted either all in one color or, more often, with woodwork one color and the wall in off-white or a contrasting color. Green remained popular, especially yellow-green and medium to dark blue-green. Other colors used were blue, blue-gray, gold, red, yellow, light brown, mustard, and putty in a range from tints to medium and darker values. Faux painting imitating wood or marble was used, and floors were stenciled or covered with Oriental carpets. Hand-painted scenic wallpapers from China brought natural motifs indoors; scenic wall murals and

Opposite: The crimson drawing room at Syon sheds the architectural look of columns and marble in previous rooms, and color is provided by silk wall covering and a carpet designed by Adam. Some reference is made to the entrance hall—the paterae in the coved ceiling of the apse are repeated in the drawing room in the multicolored pattern of the painted ceiling.

Queen Anne Dining Room, Winterthur. The wall paneling comes from a mid-eighteenth-century house in New Hampshire. Pea green, a popular wall color at the time, provides a soothing background for the bold patterns on the chairs, carpet, and accessories.

Opposite: The Chinese Parlor, Winterthur. Hand-painted scenic wall-papers were popular in eighteenth-century America. Increasing trade with the Orient prompted an enthusiasm for Chinese decorative motifs. In addition to relating to the wallpaper in color, the green damask draperies have a graceful floral pattern that complements the foliage and movement in the scenic wallpaper.

Above: Baltimore Room, The Metropolitan Museum of Art. This dining room, an excellent example of an American Federal interior, comes from a Baltimore house, c.1810. The period's characteristic oval within a rectangle can be seen on the mantle and paneling in the alcoves. The furniture was made locally, while the lighting and accessories were imported from England, France, and China. Pink was a popular wall color, and painted floor cloths were a durable alternate to carpet.

portraits by itinerant painters were a less expensive option. Porcelains from Europe or the China trade provided colorful accessories.

A good example of the American classical revival style can be found in Monticello, the Virginia home of Thomas Jefferson—lawyer, statesman, author, architect, gentleman farmer, and third president of the United States. When the building first began around 1769, Palladio's Villa Pisani in Vicenza, Italy, served as inspiration for the portico. But it was Jefferson's appointment as ambassador to France in 1784 that allowed him to study the Roman temple at Nimes, where he was influenced by the purity and integrity of classic forms. This, along with ideas borrowed from French neoclassic architecture, led to extensive revisions of his plans for Monticello. Jefferson was directly involved in the interior furnishings of Monticello down to the last detail, from a collection of sculpture and historic maps to the bed alcoves he had admired in France. Archives show his sketches of curtain designs to be made "of crimson damask silk, lined with green and yellow fringe."[3]

Toward the end of the eighteenth century, numerous publications directed architecture, primarily in interiors, to a new American Federal style, which lasted until about 1820. Books on the excavations at Pompeii, interiors by Robert Adam, and furniture pattern books by the English cabinetmakers Hepplewhite and Sheraton merged to inspire a style for the new nation, along with the adoption of its own symbols, the star and the eagle.

The American version of the Adam style was simplified. Stone columns were translated to wood. Rectangles, either on furniture or in plaster relief patterns on walls, were softened with ovals, circles, and graceful swags. In some cases, the shape of a room changed as well, an example being the Oval Office in the White House. Scenic wallpapers imported from England, France, or China were popular in living and dining rooms and in entrance halls. Solid or subtly patterned wallpapers had highly festooned, decorated borders that virtually outlined the room, as they were placed above the dado, below the cornice, and around windows and doors. Floral, stripe, and small geometric patterns appeared later, as well as faux painting in imitation of marble or of mahogany on doors. Floors were covered with patterned carpet in geometric or floral designs, and the painted floor cloth, an economical option for the hall or dining room, became the forerunner of linoleum. Adam's pastel palette of rose red, blue, green, and gold was adopted, and colors later took on the strong tones of the French Directoire and Empire—bright green, ruby red, yellow, blue, and purple. China trade brought silks in bright reds and yellow, which were used for drapery or upholstery. At Mount Vernon,

3. William Howard Adams,
Jefferson's Monticello, 220.

George Washington's home in Virginia, which transitions from Georgian to Federal, walls in public rooms range from Prussian blue to deeper green and blue-green.

3

THE REGENCY PERIOD in England (1810–20) takes its name from the Prince of Wales, who ruled as regent while his father, George III, was incapacitated. During this period, which continued well into the 1830s, the Pompeian ornament of Adam evolved into the simpler forms of Greek antiquity, along with those of non-European cultures such as the Egyptian and the Turkish. The Gothic style was also reevaluated. The growing middle class wanted more modest country houses with smaller rooms, simpler wall surfaces, and scaled-down furniture. Colors paralleled the French Directoire and Empire periods with deeper reds, greens, yellow, and brown instead of pastels.

A noted architect of the period, Sir John Soane, whose house at Lincoln's Inn Fields in London contains his collection of ancient fragments, in addition to thousands of drawings by Robert Adam and his brother James, took an eclectic approach to "the poetry of architecture." He manipulated light and color in his London home by bringing sunlight into the drawing room with yellow walls, drapery, and upholstery. The library and dining room on the floor below were painted deep Pompeiian red with green trim. But most poetic is the way he brought light into the interior breakfast room by placing, on slender piers, an umbrellalike dome with a scattering of mirrors to create a fragmented effect of light.

By 1820 in America, the Greek Revival style of architecture filtered into interiors with the appearance of architectural columns, while the migration of French cabinetmakers brought the Empire influence to furniture. Although wallpaper above the wainscot was still popular, wainscoting started to disappear, baseboards grew heavier, and walls become a more neutral off-white, gray, or neutralized pink or terra cotta. By this time, walls were usually plaster, in one color from floor to ceiling. Ongoing furnishing at the White House reflected the Empire influence in the bright, clear colors of the Red, Blue, and Green Rooms.

The nineteenth century saw rapid growth in science and technology, from the development of the Jacquard loom for machine-made textiles and carpet, to the first transatlantic crossing by steamship, to the invention of the railway, telegraph, photographic process, sewing machine, telephone, phonograph, electric lamp, and motor car. When Queen Victoria ascended the throne of England in 1837, expansion in manufacturing industries and increase in travel was leading to the growth of cities and the creation of new towns, as well as to the emergence of a large, prosperous middle class with an increasing desire for furnishings. Choices were abundant, and ideas were borrowed from all periods—Gothic, Renaissance, baroque, rococo, and non-European cultures—often mixed with little or no thought. The use of the machine lowered production costs, and manufacturers sought to increase sales with frequent intro-

The Nineteenth Century and Beyond

ductions of new designs. Good taste and craftsmanship were sadly diminished, and the overuse of ornament with little thought to function resulted in homes that were severely cluttered.

Augustus Welby Pugin, who worked as an architect on the Houses of Parliament, published books extolling Gothic architecture in 1836 and 1841,[1] which provided a foundation for the Gothic Revival. Pugin examined the ethical connection between architecture and society, comparing the classical and medieval past in terms of aesthetic and moral values. John Ruskin, an architect and critic, carried on the ideas of Pugin but focused more on aesthetic principles and the appropriate use of ornament. He believed that objects made by machine, without the creative hand of the craftsman, lacked true value, and that design, instead of being a constant search for new forms, could be inspired by knowledge of history and nature.

The 1851 International Exposition in London, the first major exhibition of industrial products and crafts from around the world, showed arts and crafts from other countries to be superior to English products in design and color. A huge Crystal Palace of pre-fabricated parts, designed by Joseph Paxton, was set up in Hyde Park—a combination of iron and glass that resembled a greenhouse. Ruskin was critical of the machine-made, uniform components, never realizing they forecast the future of building. The interior was painted by Owen Jones—an architect, decorator, and major organizer of the Exposition—in the clear primary colors of the "classical tradition."

In 1856, Owen Jones published *The Grammar of Ornament*, a study of color and pattern styles of nineteen world cultures and historic periods, including the lesser-known "Ornament of Savage Tribes" plus a chapter on natural foliage. Like Ruskin, Jones provided two sources of inspiration for the designer—history and nature—not to be copied, but to be interpreted creatively in order to develop new forms. Jones traveled to Italy and France, as well as to Egypt, Greece, and Turkey. He was so intrigued by Islamic architecture that he made the first detailed study of the Alhambra in Granada, Spain, and later wrote of the Moorish palace, "The grace and refinement of Greek ornament is here surpassed."[2] He saw that the Moors had used color in accordance with the laws of nature by which color defines form, observing that, "The ancients always used colour to assist in the development of form, always employed it as a further means of bringing out the constructive features of a building."[3] He gives as an example a plant, where the leaf is one color, the flower another, and the earth in which it stands a third color.

In spite of the concern over the use of the machine and poor craftsmanship, the habits of manufacturers and consumers were slow to change. Furniture was ornate, and large, upholstered chairs and ottomans bore swags and oversized fringes. Windows

1. These are listed in *The New Columbia Encyclopedia* as "Contrasts," 1836, and "The True Principles of Pointed or Christian Architecture," 1841.

2. *The Grammar of Ornament*, 206, 208. The quote is from Owen Jones's catalog for the Crystal Palace. Jones's study, "Plans, Elevations, Sections and Details of the Alhambra" (1836–45), was published in two volumes.

3. Ibid, Chapter 10, Proposition 10: "Moresque Ornament from The Alhambra," 196.

Page 46: Detail of the Barcelona Pavilion (pp. 60–61)
Above: The Ballantine House, Newark. The library of the 1885 restored Victorian mansion incorporates a mixture of decorative influences. The upper walls are made of plaster painted red and decorated with metal leaf. A portion of the stained-glass window, which reflects the emerging Art Nouveau style and is attributed to the Tiffany studios, can be seen.

could have as many as four layers of drapery, eliminating daylight; bold patterns in wallpaper and carpeting added to the visual complexity. One good thing that came out of the textile industry was the range of brightly colored floral chintz and paisley patterns originating in India, which have contributed to good interiors to this day.

The Victorian age saw rooms assigned to specific activities, and the rooms could be treated differently in design and decoration. For example, the rococo style might be followed in the drawing room or bedroom, and Gothic in the library or dining room of the same house.[4] Mass-produced wallpaper was popular, and came in floral and geometric patterns or flocked or embossed to imitate cut-velvet or leather. Different papers were used on upper and lower portions of the wall. Walls were topped with colorful borders or a stenciled pattern on the frieze below the crown molding. Grand houses had stone and marble or parquet floors; wall-to-wall pile carpet was reserved for more formal rooms.

Wood was generally dark—oak, mahogany, rosewood, ebony, or black walnut. Furniture was also made from papier-mâché with mother-of-pearl inlay to give an illusion of cloisonné. Popular colors early in the period were deep and rich red, pink, and green, as well as blue, in a transition from the Regency or Empire. Later colors tended to be drab and heavy—maroon, olive green, dark purple, brown, gold, and black—and this morose effect was intensified by the limitations of gaslight. Analine purple, or mauve, a dye discovered in 1856, became the color most identified with the Victorian period. Later discoveries produced brilliant magenta, blue, green, and yellow.

The Arts and Crafts movement brought a major change to interiors. William Morris (1834–96), best known for his still-popular textile and wallpaper designs, was a writer and social reformer who, trained as an artist, led an attempt to unite the decorative arts and architecture to restore taste. His efforts would eventually lead to an identifiable new style. As a young man, Morris had visited the Gothic cathedrals in France. He admired the mellow colors of faded tapestries as well as the stained-glass windows that were to become part of his interiors. He believed in honesty in design, in letting materials be what they are, and was against machine production in favor of handmade crafts to regain the skill and spiritual input of the craftsman. He drew directly from nature's forms of fruit, flowers, foliage, and animals, but his patterns were stylized and two-dimensional. In 1861, he was a founding partner in a firm that later became Morris & Co., which designed, manufactured, and sold all household furnishings—textiles, wallpaper, furniture, stained glass, pottery, metalwork, and tapestries. Natural dyes were used on hand-blocked cotton chintzes and on wall-

In the upper landing of Red House, William Morris combined the modern and medieval, with plain white walls at a time when Victorian rooms were dark and cluttered, and a painted stencil pattern on the ceiling.

4. Mary Gilliatt, *Period Style*, 112.

paper; woolen textiles were handwoven; and cushions or fire screens were embroidered by hand.

Arts and Crafts interiors had lower ceilings, often with exposed beams. The windows were small, and stained glass was revived. The dado could line up with chair height, or it could be raised to shoulder height or higher, or the room could be completely paneled, as was common in dining rooms. Morris preferred plain, whitewashed walls over poorly designed wall covering, a startling idea at the time. Chintzes were popular and were used on windows the year round instead of as a summer drapery; the lighter colors gave them a more contemporary feel, a trend that has continued. Textiles and wallpaper ranged from lighter, natural colors, like faded tapestries, to darker, neutralized blues, a range of greens, browns, purple, and ocher, often freshened by the use of white or light neutrals.

When Japan opened its borders to trade in the mid-nineteenth century, Westerners were astonished that, because of its isolation, the arts of this feudal country were suspended in a time comparable to medieval Europe. Another surprise was the spareness and simplicity of Japanese design in a period when Victorian products were covered with ornament. Christopher Dresser (1834–1904), who illustrated the natural foliage plates for Jones's *Grammar of Ornament*, became one of the most prescient and influential designers of the period in his abstraction or stylization of forms and his belief in utility and function. In addition to admiring Jones's work on Islamic art, Dresser was intrigued by Japanese art; while others may have looked upon it as a novelty, he perceived its underlying spiritual force. Although he shared many of Morris's views, Dresser was the more optimistic of the two, believing that man and machine could work together to create good design—an idea ahead of its time.

In 1876, Dresser was invited by the Japanese government to visit the country and review its industries. He was greatly impressed by the subtle and restrained use of color in Japanese interiors, where neutral backgrounds were energized by colorful, painted screens or smaller accessories such as porcelains. He applied these principles to his interiors by using muted colors and patterns for carpets and walls in order to provide a neutral background for the furniture. His definition of neutral varied, but his ideal was to observe from afar the vibrant "bloomy" effect created when nature crowded together flowers of all colors.[5] He felt it was a designer's responsibility to raise the level of the client's taste by becoming a teacher of art and explaining the reasons for design decisions and their successful outcome.

At the turn of the century, Frank Lloyd Wright carried the Arts and Crafts tradition from England to America. He was able to combine Western and non-Western traditions

---

5. Christopher Dresser, *Principles of Victorian Decorative Design*, 46. Dresser further states that bright primary and secondary colors could be used in smaller quantities, along with neutrals such as black and white, to create a similar effect

(he admired the simplicity of Japanese prints) to come up with a unique style of architecture, and he designed every aspect of his buildings, including furniture and lighting; he even designed textiles. Unlike Morris, Wright approved of the machine, which he felt did some work better than the hand, especially with new construction materials.

The Twentieth Century

With the approach of the twentieth century, European artists and designers sought a new style to reflect the modern world; instead of going back to traditional forms, they created a new decorative style, Art Nouveau, using natural forms. Although it was short-lived, perhaps because, like the baroque, the excessive movement of its curves became tiresome, Art Nouveau forged an important link between the nineteenth and twentieth centuries. Interiors continued the trend initiated by Morris. Walls were light, and colors were softer than earlier, and related to natural earth tones, combining muted reds, orange, and yellow with leafy greens and blue, browns, and warm woods.

Another movement was taking place in Vienna, where artists—among them, Gustav Klimt—broke away from restrictions imposed by the academy to organize their own exhibitions and form the Secessionist movement in 1897. The Austrian architect Josef Hoffmann, an early member, was sympathetic to the ideals of craftsmanship and went on to found the Wiener Werkstätte, which sought to unite artist and craftsman in order to produce good design, in 1903. In Brussels, he designed a townhouse for Adolphe Stoclet to hold a collection of antique and modern art; Hoffmann adhered to the ideals of impeccable craftsmanship and to designing everything in a building on a grand and luxurious scale, from the architecture and the interiors down to the tea service. The Palais Stoclet (1905–11), as it was called, was completely unique: pristine, white, and geometric. The openness and lightness of materials, highly polished glass and marble, and simple lines and planes were utterly opposite to Art Nouveau. Marble, ranging in color from dark green to warm, creamy whites to black, was used freely on the interior walls, and giant mosaics by Gustav Klimt were set between marble walls in the dining room.

Art Nouveau was to last only about twenty years; the pendulum of taste swung from curved lines back to classic forms, but these would be interpreted in an entirely different way because of new technology and building materials. The concept of quality products was still alive, but instead of their being made by an artist/craftsman, now it was artist, craftsman, and industry working together that created a product of quality and affordability.

Overleaf: Palais Stoclet, Josef Hoffmann. The sharp contrast of dark and light is muted by the warmth of the cream colored marble walls as well as the dining table. The large wall mosaics by Gustav Klimt provide a touch of color, and the tendrils in their tree motif complement the graining of the marble but contrast with the geometric planes of walls and furniture.

L'Exposition Internationale des Arts Décoratifs et Industriels Modernes, held in Paris in 1925, was intended to display the most modern French furniture and decorative work. The term "Art Deco" was derived from this exhibition, although at the time the style was known as "style moderne." In America, Art Deco took on a commercial association in the design of skyscrapers, airplanes, ocean liners, stores, theaters, and hotels. Industrial design was born, and new electrical appliances were given modern, streamlined forms.

Ancient civilizations again provided inspiration for this new movement. The stepped-back profile of Mayan temples reappeared in the stepped forms of tall buildings and furniture. Discovery of the tomb of the ancient Egyptian ruler Tutankhamen in 1922 with its riches intact furnished a treasure of design motifs and colors—ochers, turquoise, lapis blue, and gold.

The French architect Le Corbusier, who in 1923 had written that "a house is a machine for living in," exhibited his work at the 1925 Exposition's Pavillon d'Espirit Nouveau, but his furniture and modular cabinets received less attention than the work of Émile-Jacques Ruhlmann, one of the most prominent furniture designers of the era. Taking a disciplined approach to the scale, grace, proportion, and execution of furniture, Ruhlmann designed motifs that were abstract and geometric but still decorative. Even with new materials and some machine production, he used fine, rare woods such as macassar ebony, shagreen, and ivory and tortoiseshell for insets.

Ruhlmann also designed complete interiors, which, although always luxurious, were as varied as his furniture. Some of his interiors were calm, with the warmth and subtle textures of dark woods set against light neutral walls, simple silk draperies, plain leather or velvet upholstery, and a touch of chrome or bronze; other rooms might be wildly ornate, with patterned wall coverings, draperies, carpet, and giant murals. All carried his distinct signature.

The seeds of Art Deco may be found in cubism and other progressive art movements, the growing interest in the work of architects such as Josef Hoffmann, and the influence of Russian music and folklore, after the impresario Serge Diaghilev brought his Ballets Russes to Paris in 1909. At the opening performance of a ballet set in eighteenth-century France, the legendary dancer Vaslav Nijinsky stunned the audience in a shimmering costume of "white, yellow, and silver" against a background "in the colors of Sèvres porcelain." Another ballet, *Scheherazade*, featured astonishing color combinations—red with orange; pink, gold, and black with green and blue; bronze, silver, pearls, and lamé—that were to change the look of fashion and interiors.[6]

---

6. Suzanne Massie, *Land of the Firebird*, 433, 437.

Notable homes and interiors in Paris in the Art Deco period heralded a move toward the modern. One house by Robert Mallet Stevens built in 1926–27—with a composition of pristine exterior planes of white with a bright red band on top, yellow window shades, and the energetic diagonal of a black stair rail following steps to an upper terrace—resembles an abstract painting. The entire facade of the Maison de Verre (Glass House, 1928–32) by Pierre Chareau is of prefabricated panels of glass. For this combined doctor's office and residence, Chareau designed everything, down to the furniture, hardware, and coatracks, with a great deal of attention to the function and comfort of the owner; the neutral palette gave the interior a contemporary feel.

In 1919—in a move that grew out of the 1907 Deutsche Werkbund, a society of artists established in Germany to raise the level of design in industry—the German government at Weimar founded the Bauhaus, a school that would combine teaching the fine arts and applied arts. Under the direction of architect Walter Gropius, students received training in design theory and color, as well as hands-on production as apprentices in various workshops under a faculty of artists, architects, and craftsmen. The most innovative exploration of new materials came out of the furniture workshop under Marcel Breuer, who started as an apprentice and later became the workshop's director. Plastic, tubular steel, and laminated plywood were all used to make practical furniture with standard components that would be economical to manufacture and easy to assemble.

Innovation and new interpretation of old materials was also the aim in the stained-glass, metal, and weaving workshops. Upholstery fabric was double-woven for durability; stained-glass windows by Josef Albers and carpets that came out of the weaving workshop took on the colors and expression of abstract art.

Along with these developments, a new type of architecture emerged, which grew out of the classic tradition and was based on clear, simple forms. The term "International Style" was derived from a 1932 exhibit at the Museum of Modern Art in New York, which featured the work of architects of the 1920s whose styles based on pure geometric forms were not identifiable with any culture or country. New materials would dictate the style, as they did in earlier periods.[7] Machine production had contributed to the creation of a new society whose buildings were practical, functional, and economical, but with a measure of spiritual quality and refinement. Buildings became lighter and more transparent and took on a different texture with reflective glass and metal. The gloss of these modern materials extended to furniture as well, while natural materials such as marble and wood became major sources of interior color.

7. The name is taken from a book published at the time of the exhibit—*The International Style: Architecture Since 1922*, by Henry-Russell Hitchcock and Philip Johnson.

Ludwig Mies van der Rohe (1886–1969), a name virtually synonymous with modern architecture, was in his early years an admirer of the work of the great nineteenth century neoclassic architect Karl Schinkel. In his residential projects, Mies was sympathetic with a movement to promote better health by bringing light and air into the home, as well as by providing a garden, however small. The new technology of steel and glass gave him the freedom not only to bring nature indoors, but also to extend the living area outdoors, initiating a completely new concept of interior space. The landscape became part of the interior, like a painting on the wall, with the architect framing the view.

At the 1929 International Exposition in Barcelona, Mies designed the German Pavilion, a dazzling composition of simple, reflective planes and surfaces of polished green marble and onyx, tinted and clear glass, and chrome-covered columns and mullions. Indoors and outdoors were connected through the glass walls with a continuous travertine floor. The geometric grid was broken by a female statue and graceful chairs—which became known as "Barcelona chairs"—whose leather seats and backs rested on steel bases composed of intersecting curves. Dividing the main room was an onyx wall, its contrasting bands arranged in an almost complete diamond pattern, which highlighted the jewellike quality of the mineral and made it a focal point of the interior.

Mies used a similar approach in a private commission the same year, the Tugendhat House in Brno, Czech Republic. The living area, overlooking the landscape, was divided by a polished onyx wall, while an ebony wall partially circled the dining area, the textures of onyx and ebony contrasting with silk draperies and polished chrome columns. In addition to the gardens, Mies considered furniture and its placement an extension of his architecture. This new style of house, although appealing to many clients, was not without critics. There were issues of privacy and security in the open plan and, even with draperies, a transparency akin to living outdoors; and there were no walls on which to hang paintings or photographs.

History reveals a constant cycle of change and adaptation. With advances in construction techniques that allowed greater window openings, the dwelling became more transparent, forever changing our perception of color and light. The steel and glass technology of the twentieth century removed the barrier of walls to give new freedom and present panoramic views of landscape or city. These real views would gradually replace the historic decoration and embellishment of interior walls. In today's homes, whether urban or suburban, traditional or modern, the electronic age, by means of television and the computer, has brought even more of the world indoors. Nevertheless, the fact that people still build and restore traditional homes and collect antiques reveals an ongoing need for a connection with the past.

Overleaf: The Barcelona Pavilion.

2

COLOR
THEORY
AND
MEANING

IN A *NEW YORK TIMES* ARTICLE detailing the challenges faced by NASA in the design of the space station, color was cited as one of the many factors critical to the physical and emotional well-being of the crew. On a long space flight, energy conservation was a priority, and in order to provide maximum reflective surfaces, walls in the space station were white. The commander of the 1974 Skylab crew, who later became a consultant to the program, recalled that the "astronauts aboard [his] ship were so starved for color they would stare at the test color bars used to calibrate their cameras" and wanted "more texture to relieve the eye."[1]

More than a century earlier, in his book *The Principles of Decorative Design*, Christopher Dresser wrote, "With form our very nature seems to demand colour." He went on to imagine what it would be like if land, water, and sky were all the same color: "There would be no green to cheer, no blue to soothe, no red to excite . . ."[2] Nature has always provided the visual stimulation of color, light, and texture, while history has shown the human need for variety and change: the eighteenth-century neoclassical period favored the pastels of spring; designers of the Victorian and Art Nouveau periods in the nineteenth century used floral patterns, lush vines, and the foliage of summer; the early twentieth century brought the autumn colors favored by Frank Lloyd Wright, and moved on to beige; the century closed with the neutral whites of winter.

Early Symbolism

While we often think of color as one-dimensional—something merely applied to a surface—archaeological studies demonstrate the depths of color's religious and symbolic significance. Black, white, and red were the colors used in the most ancient cultures and are prominent to this day. Evidence of red ocher spread on Neanderthal graves suggests that people associated the color red with life-giving blood and perhaps the hope of rebirth, as nature was reborn in the cycle of the seasons. The word stems from the Sanskrit word for blood *rudhira*. The American Indian associated red with the south or day, and black, the night.[3] In the book *Colour*, by Donald Pavey *et alii*, a theory is suggested that other colors such as green and yellow became significant only after the transition to agriculture as a means of food, and that this transition may have caused a shift in the meaning of black to life, as dark soil gave birth to new plant life. Black, white, and red were also woven in the legendary phoenix (stemming from *phoinix*, the Greek word for purple or crimson), the Egyptian bird consumed by fire and arising from its dark ashes to the light of rebirth.

Gold or red symbolized the rising or setting sun, which was worshipped as a source of life by ancient civilizations from the Mayans of Mexico to the Aztecs in Peru to the

Symbolism to Psychology

Page 64: Navajo wool blanket c. 1860–70, Arizona or New Mexico. Black, white, and red, as well as earth tones, were the earliest colors of primitive societies and are prominent in some cultures to this day.

Above: Achaemenian gold bowl (522–404 BC, Iran). Gold, ancient symbol of the sun and gods, has been a symbol of wealth and power throughout history. Even when crafted into simple forms, its radiance is universally appealing.

Egyptians, whose pharaoh was considered a descendent of the sun god Ra. Gold, which represented the sun's brilliant rays, was used in the decoration of tombs and temples, funerary masks, jewelry, and statues. On a papyrus depicting funeral rites, Shu, god of air, was shown holding a red sun disk above his head. The golden circle of light, or nimbus, around a saint's head in early Christian mosaics and icons and in later paintings represented divine power and enlightenment. Gold has been used for royal crowns and symbols of authority throughout history. Louis XIV was called the "Sun King" not only because of his power as an absolute monarch, but also for the dazzling opulence of his palaces and court.

As the golden rays of sun were life-giving, the color red was used to restore life through healing.[4] Colored gems and amulets were used in the treatment of diseases as well as for protection from evil, and they provided the basis for some of our color associations today. To the Egyptians, red was for protection from fire as well as for treatment of disease, green was for fertility, yellow for prosperity, blue for faith, and white for divine protection. The Greeks also connected color with cures. Pythagoras supposedly used color as well as poetry and music to treat illness. Red plasters were prescribed by Celsus for bleeding and saffron yellow to ease the mind.[5] Magical powers were also assigned to gems by ancient civilizations: sapphire, representing the blue sky, for bodily healing and mental composure; ruby to avoid disease; and emerald for wisdom, as well as for the treatment of eye problems, a practice that carried over to the green lines and background of accounting ledgers used before the advent of computers.

Color symbolism was prominent in the Bible and early Christianity: red stood for compassion or martyrdom, blue for divinity, white for purity and joy, green for immortality, yellow or gold for celestial glory, and purple for sorrow. The trinity of father, son, and holy ghost was represented by blue, yellow, and red. The brilliance of a color was important, as in Ezekiel's comparison of the throne of God to the color of a blue sapphire.[6]

Just as gems were considered a cosmic source of color, ancient civilizations ascribed color to the planets as well as to the elements and direction of the compass. The Greeks recognized the four elements of matter to be earth, air, fire, and water, symbolized by green, yellow, red, and blue. The Chinese added a fifth element, metal, and associated four colors plus black and white with the four seasons and compass directions: to the north was black, representing winter and water of bottomless depth; to the south was red, for summer, representing fire; to the east, blue and green for spring, representing wood and its new growth; to the west, white, for autumn and the color of metal; and in the center was the earth, in yellow.[7] Roofs in the ancient city of

1. Phil Patton, "Lost in Space: Living Room for the Crew," *The New York Times*, Sept. 8, 1994.
2. Christopher Dresser, *Principles of Victorian Decorative Design*, 30.
3. Faber Birren, *Color, A Survey in Words and Pictures*, 15.

4. The Color Association of the United States, *CAUS News*, Sept. 2003. In its "*Interiors 2005/2006 Forecast*," designer Sharon Clarke-Fodor reports a trend to "reds and mauves" in the health care market.
5. Faber Birren, *Color, A Survey*, 40, 56.
6. Ibid., 33, 37

7. C. Thomas Mitchell, and Jiangmei Wu, *Living Design: The Daoist Way of Building*, 13. Also Donald Pavey et al., *Colour*, 59. In China, white as a symbol of mourning may be its connection to the west and to "metal, the deadliest element."

Peking were painted yellow as protection from evil spirits. Chinese dynasties were also represented by royal colors.

Because most evidence of color used by the ancient Greeks has been erased by the elements, much of our information is derived from literature. From the writings of Pythagoras, there is evidence of white as a symbol for the divine, blue for truth, and red for both sacrifice and love. Aristotle believed all colors derived from black and white, and he perceived colors as fixed points on a scale ranging from light, or brightness, to dark: white, red, violet, green, dark blue, and black. As a seventh color there were the alternates of yellow—between white and red, and gray—between blue and black.[8] The idea persisted to medieval times, as scholars at the time believed that air (white) mixed with space (dark) created the blueness of the sky. It may be that, owing to the high cost of pigments in ancient and medieval times, bright or highly saturated colors were valued over pale ones. The significance of aspects of color is often evidenced in other cultures as well, such as in Japan, where emphasis may be placed on whether a color is vibrant or muted, and in Africa, where nonvisual sensations such as softness, roughness, or dryness are associated with color.

The opposing forces of dark and light are part of the tradition of Islam. There is the realization that light comes from a divine source, and that without darkness one would not appreciate the light and the colors brought by its rays. Four primary colors correspond to the four elements—the earth, blue; air, yellow; fire, red; water, green—and these colors are woven into a cycle of seasons, life, and time of day. Red represents spring, morning, and childhood; yellow, summer, afternoon, and youth; green, fall, evening, and maturity; and blue, winter, night, and old age. The favored color in Islam is green, not only for its life-giving association but because it embodies all colors including their symbolic meanings—blue and yellow pigments when mixed make green, and its visual after-image is red.[9]

The use of vivid colors versus subdued or no color was historically a source of controversy. In Roman times, the elder Pliny was disturbed by the ostentation of royal purple, which was obtained at a danger to the lives of those collecting thousands of sea urchins to produce minuscule quantities of the dye. In his book, *Blue, The History of a Color,* Michel Pastoureau recounts controversies in the aesthetic use of color in Christian churches in the early Gothic period. Some viewed color as materialistic and a distraction from the true meaning of worship, while others saw it as divinity that banished darkness. Abbot Suger, who reconstructed the twelfth-century Abbey of Saint-Denis near Paris, believed the latter, and made the Biblical sapphire blue promi-

8. Robert Fuller, *Color Research and Application*, 225.
9. Nader Ardalan and Laleh Bakhtiar, *The Sense of Unity, The Sufi Tradition in Persian Architecture*, 47–50.

Opposite: Although red was the color of ancient emperors and kings, blue became a color of royalty when dyes were improved in medieval times to make blue more brilliant. This image from a manuscript illuminated by Jean Fouquet, c.1460, shows English King Edward I kneeling in homage before the French king Philippe le Bel in 1286.

nent in stained-glass windows, which up to that time had been mainly red, yellow, green, and white.

According to Pastoreau this religious association, as well as an improvement in blue dyes, played a role in blue's emergence as the color of the monarchy in France in the twelfth and thirteenth centuries. Social codes later governed the use of color—red was worn by the upper classes to represent power and authority; clerics and widows were assigned less ostentatious colors. Religious backlash toward color emerged during the Protestant Reformation in the sixteenth century: gray, brown, black and white, and dull blue were virtuous colors, whereas red was associated with papal authority.

Art and Philosophy

Established religious and symbolic approaches to color dissolved during the Renaissance, when artists began to employ a more expressive mix of pigments. In the seventeenth century, scientists also began to discard the authoritative order of tradition for a new order based on rational thinking. The most noted among them were the French philosopher and scientist René Descartes (1596–1650) and the English physicist Sir Isaac Newton (1642–1727), whose discovery that "white" light contained the spectrum of colors launched a continuing series of philosophical writings as well as studies on color from clinical scientific, psychological, and physiological viewpoints.

Poets and philosophers had their say as well. We tend to look at color as a wash of pigment on a surface; the artist and philosopher see it as another dimension entirely, affecting all the senses—taste, touch, and hearing, as well as sight. Playwrights used color terms to evoke feeling, as Shakespeare did in *Twelfth Night* in Viola's reference to a "green and yellow melancholy." Johann Wolfgang von Goethe, the German poet and writer, in his 1810 book *Theory of Colors*, was uneasy with Newton's wholly scientific approach and addressed the topic in a more personal, cultural way. He wrote, "People experience a great delight in color, generally. The eye requires it as much as it requires light." He wrote about the effect of color on the senses and about color and texture, and made observations on color in interiors as well as in attire. Goethe separated colors on the "plus" side—yellow, orange, and red—from those on the "minus" side—blue and two red-blue mixtures (which mix to purple), one with more red and one with more blue. He distinguished warm and cool colors, calling them "active" or "passive," and, with an artist's eye, he noted that a highly saturated blue could be stimulating and a softer blue calming. He also observed the receding blues of "distant mountains." Goethe called primarily blue rooms "empty and cold"; however, when blue was combined with the warmth of yellow, the resulting green was an agreeable color to live with.

Opposite, above: Conspicuous opulence is displayed in this Victorian sofa, c.1855–60, attributed to John Belter. The high contrast between the yellow silk upholstery, which takes on the sparkle of gold, and the dark rosewood frame calls attention to its intricate carving. At the same time it makes the color of the fabric seem more intense.

Opposite, lower left: Green, like yellow, can send mixed psychological messages. It is a symbol of rebirth and the abundance of nature as well as the color of money. On the other hand, it can connote jealousy or, as it leans towards yellow, illness, poison, and decay. It is often not the color itself, but its degree of brightness, its quantity, proportion, and

how it is used that makes it appealing or repellant. The pastoral theme of gardening symbols and the exquisite craftsmanship of this Sèvres vase allies it with the freshness of spring.

Opposite, lower right: Gobelins tapestry covers this chair in the Croome Court Room, 1764–71, The Metropolitan Museum of Art. Mme. de Pompadour favored the rose color that bears her name. The feminine theme is carried out not only in the rose-pink color but also by the ribbon holding the bouquet of flowers in the tapestry, which is repeated in a ribbon on the chair frame.

He was emphatic that a "blue-red," pale or in small quantities, may be suitable for dress, but a carpet of the saturated color would be impossible to live with.[9]

Most importantly, Goethe connected color with texture. A color could be regal or crass, depending on its saturation and application to different textures. He likened bright yellow to gold, its sparkling effect on satin creating an opulent look; however, when neutralized and applied to an ordinary material, it had an adverse and disturbing effect. He also noted the influence of the dyeing industry and the social aspects of color—for example, how the nobles of Venice raised the status of black attire; the French love of lively color; the bright clothing of southern Europe, which balanced the hues of its scenery; and the more neutral colors of northern climates, that seem to have been appealing under the dimmer skies.

American poet and writer Ralph Waldo Emerson (1803–82), in an essay on *Art*, expressed his philosophical views on creativity, which can apply to color as well as form. He wrote about the evolution of new art from old, and the beauty derived from the simplicity of ancient cultures. Alluding to the Oriental notion of simplicity, he believed that great ideas were conveyed by simple forms. In an essay on *Nature*, he talked about the natural cycle of "Motion and Rest."[10] We will see that this concept has parallels in Oriental philosophy and can be applied to the balance of color and non-color in living spaces.

Unlike the scientist, who more often isolates or separates colors, the artist mixes colors for a desired effect. Artists such as Wassily Kandinsky, who taught at the Bauhaus, took a spiritual approach to color and its effect on all the senses in his paintings and writings. In 1923 he sent a questionnaire to students at the Bauhaus and to some of the Weimar community asking them to assign the primary colors of red, yellow, and blue to the geometric forms of a circle, square, and triangle. Most responses assigned blue, perhaps reminiscent of the dome of the sky, to the circle; yellow to the pyramid; and red to the solidity of a square. Like Goethe, Kandinsky was fascinated with the celestial colors of yellow and blue. He compared yellow to the acidity of a lemon, which, if bright, "hurts the eye after a short time, as a high note on the trumpet hurts the ear." He described blue as a "heavenly," tranquil color but, "As it deepens toward black, it assumes overtones of a superhuman sorrow." Yellow, mixed with a little blue becomes a "sickly" green, but green in its pure form "is the most peaceful color there is." He compared red to the "spiritual vibration" of a fire, which, if too intense, becomes as painful as bleeding. The range of colors in his palette gave him the visual satisfaction equivalent to good food that could be spicy or bland; the touch of colors was like ice

---

9. Johann Wolfgang von Goethe, *Theory of Colors*, 304, 306, 310, 311, 313.

10. *Essays by Ralph Waldo Emerson*, 240, 372.

Black and white can be as expressive as color in painting, film, and photography, and as we will see later, in interiors. This Japanese ink painting captures a crow delicately perched on a branch with a few strokes; empty space is an important part of the composition.

or fire, velvet or sandpaper. White, Kandinsky wrote, "affects our psyche like a great silence . . . . Black is something extinguished . . . . Gray is toneless and immobile."[11]

In an essay on "The Elimination of Color in Far Eastern Art and Philosophy," Toshihiko Izutsu observed the cultural attitude that formed the basis for the Chinese and Japanese art of black and white ink drawing and the subtle and sophisticated use of color in what was considered a medieval society. Just as words were distilled in haiku poetry, the Zen monk was master of black and white painting, where expression was achieved with the fewest strokes of the brush and the smallest amount of ink possible. The aim was not, as in Western art, to cover the entire surface of the paper; empty space was an important part of the composition, an expression of "cosmic Loneliness." He described the simplicity of the Japanese tea ceremony in which surroundings are spare, without color or sound. The elimination of distractions heightens the senses. In silence, the faintest sounds are magnified; when color is extinguished there is a heightened appreciation of its many nuances. Likewise, nature's frugality with color at dawn and dusk or on a rainy day makes us appreciate the colors of a sunny day. Like Kandinsky's silence of white and extinction of black, the eyes feast on color after a fast.

Izutsu recounted how members of the imperial court in the Heian period (794–1185) developed a sophisticated way of creating subtle nuances of color through transparency, as descriptions of costumes in *The Tale of Gengi* reveal. Garments were layered to achieve subtle combinations found in nature. Since silk was delicately transparent, a deep red could be covered by a layer of pink to produce a "pink-plum," the "bloomy" effect so admired by Dresser. Garments could have up to a dozen layers, for example, at the sleeves, with each layer shorter than the other and in a different color to produce a subtle rainbow effect. And there were those whose color sense was so refined that they could find the deepest satisfaction in black.

In the Nō drama of the Muromachi period (1392–1573), actors, resplendent in costumes of brocade in brilliant colors and gold, played out the drama with minimal bodily movement, its discipline as difficult as that of black and white painting. Color provided the motion; nonmovement provided rest, like the emptiness of white space in the painting; and, in Izutsu's analysis, subtle movement was like "a tiny dot of black ink." Color blossomed in a most lavish way in the Momoyama period (1573–1615), when panels and screens in vivid colors of red, green, and blue and extravagant amounts of gold decorated castle rooms. In their midst, however, small, neutral rooms were set aside, ostensibly to rest the senses.

11. *Kandinsky, Complete Writings on Art:* "On the Spiritual in Art," 156–59, 181–86; "Point and Line to Plane," 591; "Color Questionnaire, 1923," 850. John Gage, *Color and Meaning*, 252.

Opposite: Noh robe, Japanese, second half of the eighteenth century. Natural motifs embroidered in silk and gold leaf were used to create luxurious costumes. These robes provide good examples of how floral and geometric patterns may be successfully combined.

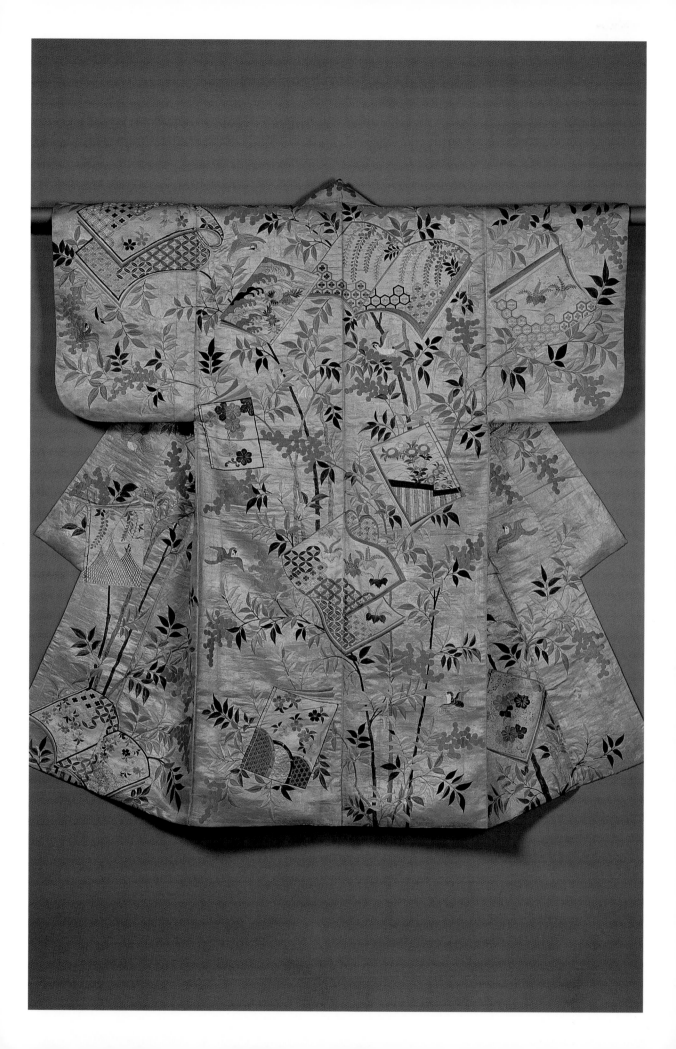

Research and Psychology

Many studies on the psychology of color have been done since Newton's time, but there are so many variables involved in conducting color research that the results in many cases may be considered less than scientific. This does not mean these studies have no merit: to psychologists they give deeper insight into the human mind; to industry they are an aid in promoting safety and efficiency; and to designers they balance the insight gained from artists, poets, and philosophers.

As with any research study, there are many questions regarding who is conducting the study and the methodology used: the personal color bias of the researcher in selecting colors and analyzing the results; the location and lighting conditions; the distraction of furnishings or the sterility of a cell-like setting; the time of day, geographic location, and climate (people may prefer warm, dark colors in winter and light pastels in summer); and the age, education, and cultural background of both the researcher and the participant.

Carl Jung, the Swiss psychologist, wrote about the "collective unconscious," where symbolic association goes far back in time, and this can apply to the individual in an association of a favorite color with an object or event. Colors that are in fashion at the time of the survey add other influences. The participant may be asked to look at and evaluate a specific color without an object in mind, but few of us are disciplined enough to do so, as people associate color with numerous visual images. People don't live in a single color environment but rather with colors in juxtaposition to each other. Proportional amounts of each color also matter. In designing a survey, how does the researcher select from thousands of colors in tints, saturations, shades, and textures, with shiny or dull surfaces?

The Swiss psychologist Hermann Rorschach used black and white ink blots, as well as color, to examine personality, emotional status, and even mental illness. In 1947 the Swiss psychologist Max Luscher developed a test for use in therapy, personnel evaluation, and medical diagnosis. Some twenty years later, eight of the seventy-three selections based on twenty-four colors in Luscher's assessment were selected for publication as a self-administered test. The colors given are identified as blue, green, red, yellow, violet, brown, gray, and black; some are light, some dark. The blue is very dark. The question arises: are we being tested on the color, or on its lightness, darkness, or saturation, which may alter perception? Similarly, the red is close to orange, the violet to rose, the brown to a neutral orange. Since test results are interpreted by placing colors in a certain sequence, one can see how perceptions might be compromised by a selection of colors that may have represented an aesthetic concept more than fifty years ago but have changed since that time.

Despite their flaws, such studies have given us interesting and useful information to balance the soul-searching, creative side of making color decisions. Surveys in Western countries have shown blue to be a favorite color, with yellow low on the list. Children respond to bright, warm colors, but this reaction changes as they get older. Studies have also reported that warm colors like red and orange tend to excite while cool colors like blue and green are more calming. This is not always true, as other studies have shown a reverse effect: red may cause an initial rise in blood pressure that is followed by a drop. Fashion editor Diana Vreeland's 1960s apartment was heavily red, but to her it was as calming as a neutral color. The one constant is that color perceptions vary as much as individuals.

Merchants and industry use psychological surveys to study the buying habits of consumers. Designers, who look at color with the eye of an artist, for its aesthetic value, are sensitive to individuals and their reactions to color but, most importantly, connect color to surface and form in order to turn a room into a pleasing composition. A balance is needed between established rules and individual creativity to solve a design problem in an intelligent but inventive way.

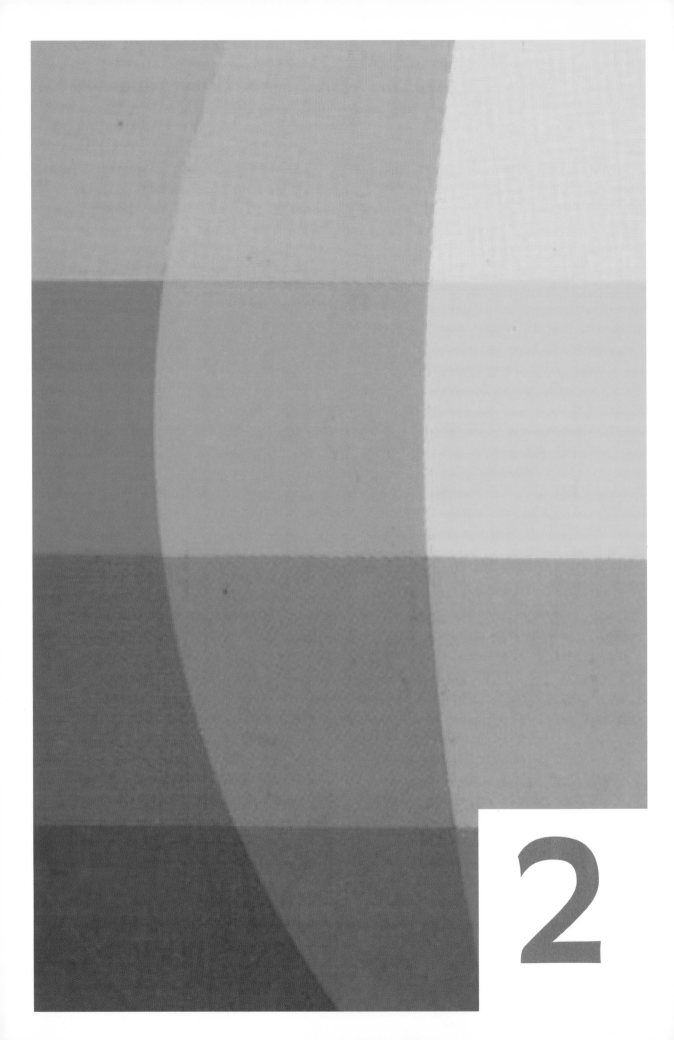

2

Light and Glass

While bringing light into the interior has always been a fundamental part of architecture, it is not certain what prompted the union of stained glass and the construction of Gothic cathedrals. With the buttress enabling a greater expanse of window, did plain glass look drab against the massive stone walls, or was there an attempt to enlarge windows to accommodate the new art form of colored glass? Did the elaborate mosaic patterns that adorned Roman floors and the walls of Byzantine churches spawn the idea of setting pieces of glass into a framework?

Earlier churches had frescoes and mosaics on their walls, which eloquently told biblical stories in jewellike colors. Now brilliantly colored glass brought bursts of color into the dark interior and replaced or, in some cases, enhanced the frescoes. The art of stained glass came to near-perfection at Chartres Cathedral in France, where the earliest windows date from the twelfth century. There was little attempt at perspective; colors—bright reds, blue, green, red-orange, and yellow—were juxtaposed for maximum pictorial effect rather than for realism, as in a scene in which a pair of green camels enter Noah's ark. Some colors were still symbolic, such as the green cross that portrayed rebirth or resurrection at both Chartres and the Abbey Church of St.-Denis. However, the earlier order of red, a symbol of light moving from a dark blue void—as seen in mosaics[1]—was reversed, and, in a twelfth-century window at Chartres, the Virgin's halo and dress are light blues against a red background. Johannes Itten (1888–1967), who taught at the Bauhaus and wrote about contrasting colors in stained glass, described the colors as "intense cold-warm contrasts" and the Virgin as "born of the primeval cosmic blue. She shines like a young star, with cold energy, surrounded by the red light of matter."[2]

In the mid-eighteenth century, there was an attempt to admit more light into the Chartres Cathedral by replacing portions of the thirteenth-century windows with clear glass, but, fortunately, this did not progress very far. The brilliance of the windows is totally dependent on daylight streaming into the almost-black interior, and too much additional light allowed into the interior would have upset this balance. This is a cautionary example of the destruction that may be caused by exchanging "modern" comforts for the moving experience of witnessing art and color in its original form.

The Separation of Light and Pigment

From earliest times, color has been tied to the sciences of astronomy and optics. Aristotle (384–322 BC) theorized on the origin of colors of the rainbow. He believed the rainbow had only three fixed, or primary colors: red, green, and blue (although yellow

Light, Color, and Visual Phenomena

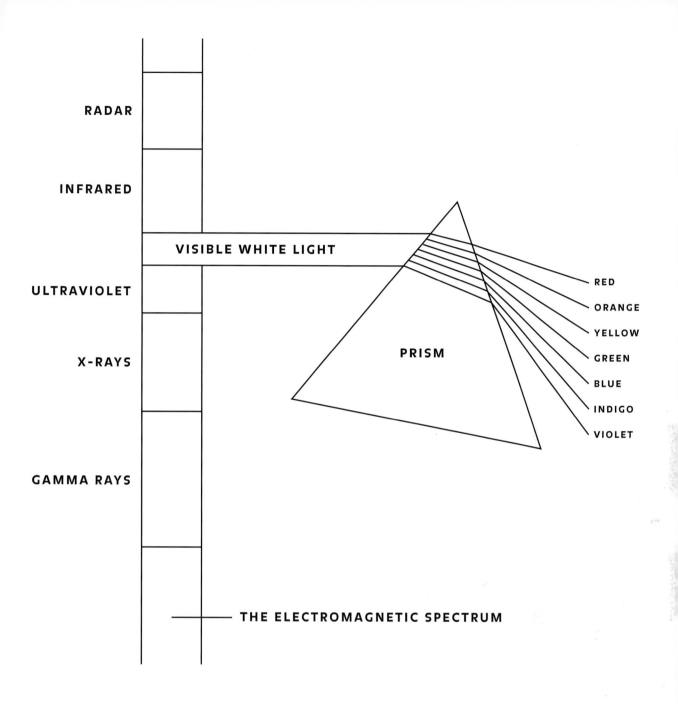

RADAR

INFRARED

VISIBLE WHITE LIGHT

ULTRAVIOLET

X-RAYS

PRISM

RED
ORANGE
YELLOW
GREEN
BLUE
INDIGO
VIOLET

GAMMA RAYS

THE ELECTROMAGNETIC SPECTRUM

Page 78: Detail of the Itten Sphere (p. 93).
Opposite: A modern interpretation of enlightenment can be seen at the National Cathedral in Washington, D.C., where a stained glass window commemorates the exploration of outer space. Centered in the red spiral is a piece of moon rock brought back by Apollo 11 astronauts.
Above: By using a prism, Newton was able to demonstrate that ordinary light could be bent, or refracted, into separate colors of different wavelengths—red having the longest and violet the shortest. Again using a prism, he was able to turn the colors back into white light.

was visible), and he assigned these three primaries to pigment as well.[3] Later an Arab scholar, Alhazen (965–1040), considered the founder of optics, conducted experiments on color and vision and also studied the geometry of the reflection and refraction of light. Around this time, the colors of the rainbow were identified as red, yellow, green, and blue.

In the early fourteenth century, Theodoric of Freiberg, a Dominican monk, wrote a treatise *On Colors* (c. 1310) and stated that the colors of the rainbow were four: red, yellow, green, and blue. He also observed the change of color in shadow but still made no distinction between the colors of light and the colors of the painter's palette, or pigment.[4]

Before Isaac Newton it was still believed that light was colorless. In his 1666 experiment of passing light through a glass prism and its refraction, Newton discovered that light contained the spectrum of colors: red, orange, yellow, green, blue, indigo, and violet. Newton also realized that mixing the entire spectrum of colors reverted back to "white" light, but he was unaware that this could also be accomplished by combining the three primary colors of light—red, blue, and green—alone. Newton's discoveries separated black and white from the colors, and brought science closer to distinguishing the colors of light from the colors of pigment. Newton organized his seven spectral colors of light into a circle whose colors are nearly complementary to each other in the pigment mixtures we know today; for example, he placed red opposite a blue and a green. A bit of a mystic as well as a scientist, Newton may have deduced seven instead of six colors from the spectrum to relate the number seven to the planets, or the notes on the musical scale, as the planets were thought by ancient astronomers to glide in harmony around the earth.

Goethe attempted to duplicate Newton's experiment with a prism but was unsuccessful; he believed that the scientific approach, while it might be helpful and even necessary at times, neglected the true beauty and psychological effect of color. Although in 1810 Goethe arranged the six colors we know as primaries (red, yellow, blue) and secondaries (orange, green, purple) in a circle according to the pigments on a painter's palette, he still held to Aristotle's view of yellow and blue as representing light and darkness.[5] At the same time, a German painter, Philipp Otto Runge, using red, yellow, and blue as primaries, developed the first color solid or sphere, with colors arranged in their progression from tints to shades. Influenced by Goethe's writings, Jan Evangelista Purkinje, a Czech scientist, began observations on color changes under different lighting conditions; in England, the artist James Northcote named dusk the "painter's hour," noting that colors painted by day took on a different character at dusk.

---

1. John Gage, *Color and Culture*, 52.

2. Johannes Itten, *The Art of Color*, 68–69.

3. Robert Feller, *Color Research and Application*, 226.

4. Ibid.

5. Goethe, *Theory of Colors*, 310; Faber Birren, *Principles of Color*, 13–14.

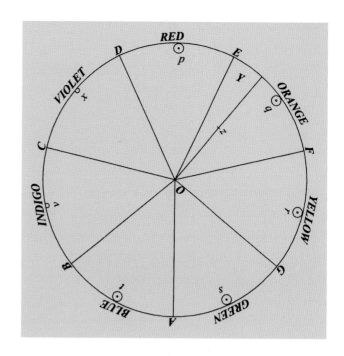

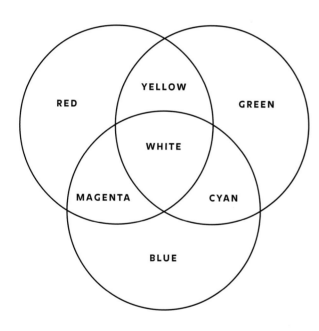

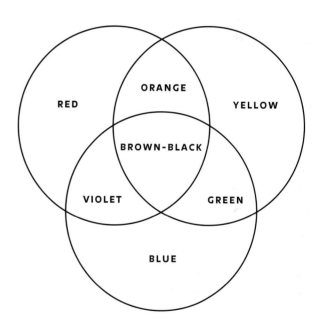

Above: Color Wheel, Sir Isaac Newton

Below, left: The additive mixtures of light.

Below, right: The subtractive mixtures of artists' pigments.

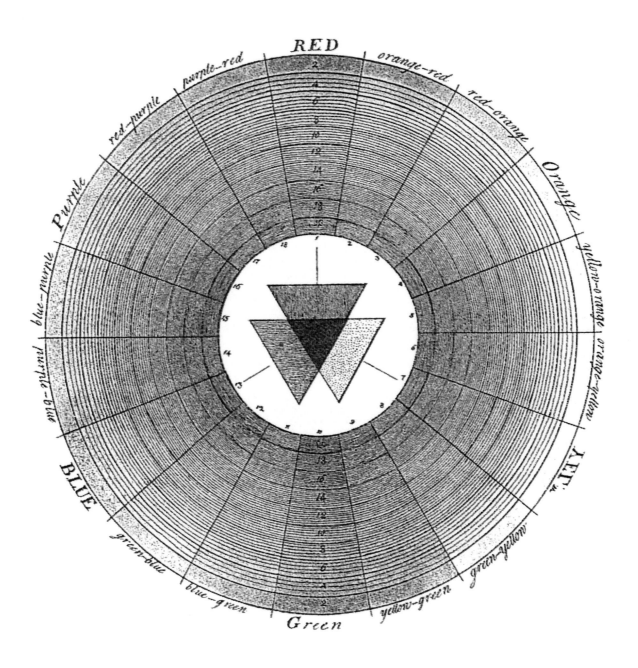

An illustration from *The Natural System of Colours* by Moses Harris,
who developed a color circle showing the mixture of primary and
secondary colors into their intermediate mixtures.

Both noticed that at dawn or dusk the reds became dark while the blues appeared lighter or brighter.[6]

The early Greeks believed that color and vision originated in the eye and that rays projected from it to strike an object and reflect back. We now know that a wide electromagnetic spectrum of energy contains invisible rays that range from short to very long: from cosmic, gamma, X-rays, ultraviolet, and infrared light to radar, radio, and television waves. In a narrow band between ultraviolet and infrared light is visible light, which contains the colors of the spectrum. Refraction occurs when a ray of light moves from one element, such as air, to a denser one, such as water or glass; its speed is slowed, and the light is bent at different angles. Red light, which contains the longest wavelength, is least refracted; violet, which contains the shortest wavelength, bends, or refracts, the most.

Leonardo da Vinci (1452–1519), in his *Treatise on Painting*, recognized the "simple colors" as white, yellow, green, blue, red, and black, in that order. He also wrote that, while white and black were not considered by some to be colors, they were essential to the painter to both receive and eliminate color. Although he considered the four colors primaries, he was aware, as a painter, that a mixture of yellow and blue pigments produced green.

In essays on the lives of artists, André Félibien, a contemporary of Newton, defined the primary colors of pigment as those that could not be obtained by mixing other colors—namely red, yellow, and blue—eliminating green, which is a mixture of yellow and blue.[7] Thus the four perceptual colors of the past—red, yellow, blue, and green—were on their way to becoming separated into two categories: the primaries of light and those of pigment. The primaries of light—red, blue, and green—are "additive." When mixed they form "white light." These primaries can be combined into secondaries—red and blue to make magenta, blue and green to make cyan, red and green to make yellow—and these colors will also, when mixed, combine into white light. The primary colors of artists' pigment—red, yellow, and blue—can be mixed to form secondaries—red and yellow to orange, yellow and blue to green, blue and red to violet. They are said to be "subtractive," because, when mixed, they will combine to form a brownish black, thus subtracting color.

In the early eighteenth century, Jacques Le Blon, a French printer, was the first to reproduce pictures using the three subtractive primaries of red, yellow, and blue. Today's printing, still a subtractive process of inks, uses four colors: magenta, yellow, cyan, and black. In 1766, Moses Harris, an English engraver, published the first full-

6. John Gage, *Color and Meaning*, 16.
7. Robert Feller, *Color Research and Application*, 222–23.

color wheel of primaries and secondaries of pigment, to which he added and identified their intermediate mixtures, obtained by mixing primary colors with adjacent secondaries.

The Eye and Color

The color of an object is visible by a process called selective absorption; that is, when white light falls on an object, certain wavelengths of color are absorbed, while others are reflected. The color we see is the color that is reflected; all others are absorbed.

The process by which the eye apprehends color is often compared to the working of a camera. On the outer layer, the cornea, which is transparent, admits light into the eye through the lens. The lens focuses images on the retina, at the back of the eye. The iris, the color portion of the eye, controls the amount of light that enters the eye through the pupil, an opening in its center. The retina contains the fovea, the area of best color response and clearest vision; it also holds two sets of light-sensitive nerves, the cones, which function for daylight vision, and the rods, which function primarily during the night and have no color response.

There are three classes of cones, each containing a different color receptor—red, blue, and green—all of which must function for normal color vision. Color blindness or deficiencies result when one or more of these are lacking. For example, to an eye without green receptors, red and green will appear similar.

The eye adjusts to a changing environment. In moving from a dark to a light room, the eye will adjust quickly; in moving from a very light to a dark room, the adjustment will take much longer. Because of its high visibility both day and night, yellow is used for warning signs and cautionary tape.

The amount of light that is reflected back to the eye determines the luminance of an object or surface. A black wall painted in a matte finish may absorb 95% light, while a white wall only 15%; glossy finishes will absorb less light, as light bounces off a reflective surface. The eye is most comfortable in a room having a range of lighting, with a higher level for specific task areas and lower levels where the eye can rest. Medieval manuscript illustrators were aware that constant focus on a white page strained their eyes and used soft green cloth to rest them.

Although a change of light will alter colors, their recognizability under varying conditions is called "color constancy." For example, white or black will be recognized as what they are in bright or dim light. Blue will be recognized as blue in daylight, candlelight, or incandescent light, although the color will change under different lights. The eye will also stress the similarity between separated colors, such as a green sofa and

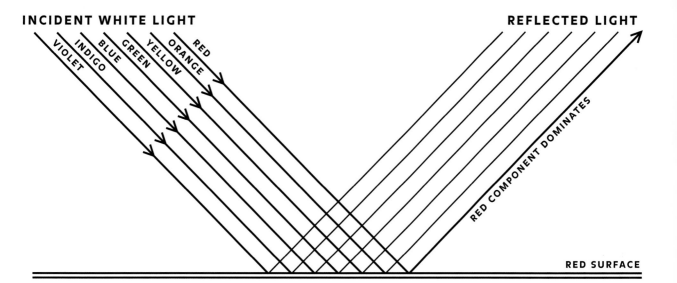

INCIDENT WHITE LIGHT

VIOLET
INDIGO
BLUE
GREEN
YELLOW
ORANGE
RED

REFLECTED LIGHT

RED COMPONENT DOMINATES

RED SURFACE

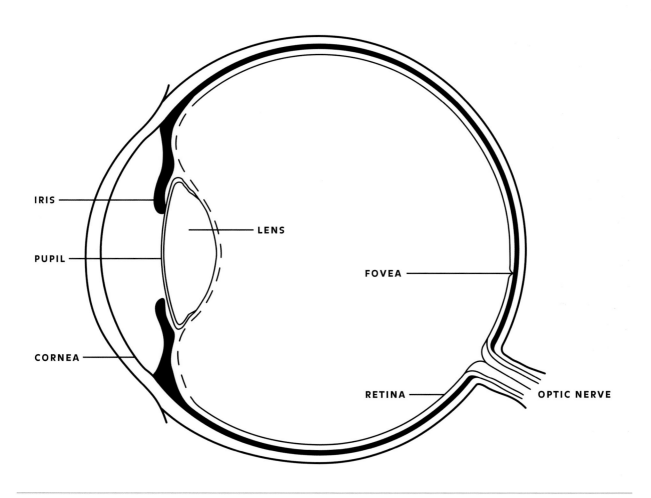

IRIS

PUPIL

CORNEA

LENS

FOVEA

RETINA

OPTIC NERVE

Above: When white light, which contains all colors of the spectrum, strikes a surface, all colors are absorbed except the color we see, which is reflected. The occurrence is known as "selective absorption."
Below: The eye shown in section.

Placing a straight edge alongside the vertical lines will show they are straight, not curved. The distortion is visual, caused by the radiating lines in the background. Theorists have likewise demonstrated that colors that are adjacent to or that overlap each other will also undergo visual illusions such as changes in tonal or chromatic value, or may appear to advance or recede. (*Color Fundamentals*, 105)

a green chair opposite it, even though the colors do not match exactly. The difference in color will be noticed when they are placed next to each other. People see color differently for many reasons. The absorption of wavelengths of light by the eye may vary slightly, or age may be a factor by causing the eye's structures to yellow, making blue more difficult to match.

Colors that match under one light source, but not another, are called a "metameric" match. Matching is best done in daylight, which contains the full spectrum of colors. Colors should always be checked as well under the interior artificial lighting that will be used. Incandescent lamps are higher in warm wavelengths and may cast a yellowish light, while some fluorescent lamps are cool and will cast a bluish light; either one can make colors that are attractive by day look unappealing by night. Pastel tints can also fade out under low lighting conditions.

Color Phenomena and Visual Perception

The greatest leap in the study of color was made in the early nineteenth century by a French chemist, M. E. Chevreul, who was called upon to restore quality control to the Gobelins tapestry works. When Chevreul became director of dyes in 1824, Gobelins's black dyes seemed off, and the violets, blues, and grays appeared to be unstable. Noting that the colors of the dyed yarn were correct before the yarn was woven, Chevreul realized that the problem was due to the juxtaposition of colors after weaving. He began experiments with color phenomena that revolutionized the study of color for both artist and scientist. His book, *The Principles of Harmony and Contrast of Colors*, published in 1839, was later updated with comments by the twentieth-century color theorist Faber Birren.

Chevreul began with Newton's seven colors of the spectrum, but as mixtures of dyes or pigments, not of light; he later eliminated indigo. He listed the subtractive primaries and secondaries as we know them—red, yellow, blue, orange, green, and violet. His seventy-two-color circle was based on primaries and secondaries with their intermediate mixtures; that is, red was followed by five increasing steps of red mixed with orange to achieve a grading to red-orange. The circle followed the painter's palette, with red and green as complements opposite each other. Chevreul also envisioned colors with their range of tints, shades, and neutralized values in a hemisphere.

Chevreul's research revealed that the problem with the Gobelins dyes was not a chemical one but one of visual perception, since the eye reads colors differently depending on what colors are near them. He found that colors seen together will affect each other in different ways: making them appear darker or lighter, taking on the tinge of another color, becoming brighter or more neutral, or, if small enough, canceling each other and dissolving into gray. His discovery of the "law of simultaneous contrast of colors" provided a "means of assorting colored objects so as to obtain the best possible effect from them, according to the taste of the person who combines them."[8]

The law of simultaneous contrast states that when colors of different values are placed side by side, the contrast of the two will make the darker one appear darker, while the lighter color will look lighter. Added to this is another phenomenon, successive contrast or after-image, in which each color will take on the visual complement of the other to further change its appearance. As an example, if one stares at a red disk on a white ground and then shifts the focus away from it to white, a green after-image will appear.

Although red, green, and blue were not yet recognized as the primaries of light, Chevreul was aware that complementary mixtures were taking place within the eye. He demonstrated that when pure gray was placed next to different colors, the gray not only took on a slight tint of the color's complement but also changed in value, for example, appearing lighter on a purple background, and darker on yellow. When complementary colors such as red and green were placed side by side, both colors appeared brighter; the green after-image of red was projected on the green and raised its intensity, and vice versa.

Chevreul went a step further in studying this juxtaposition by changing the proportions of yarns to visually alter colors. He warned, however, that using complementary colors together did not always heighten their appearance, for when woven together in small proportions they ran the risk of "extinguishing each other." Further experiments by the Scottish scientist James Clerk Maxwell showed how colors could be mixed visually by spinning them on a disk.

In studying stained-glass windows, Chevreul noted how separating colors by outlining them with black added to their brilliance and defined the color even at a distance. He was very much aware of the effects of sunlight and candlelight on color and staged experiments in color constancy.

Chevreul's laws on the harmony of colors have influenced both artists and designers. His first law was just to observe and admire a single color against a white background; the second was to look at the range of a single color in a scale from tints to shades; the third, to observe the harmony in the contrast of adjacent colors while avoiding having the two "injure each other" by lowering the value of one to heighten the other; the fourth, to observe the harmony of complementary colors; the fifth, to view the harmony of a dominant hue in a field of colors.

---

8. M.E. Chevreul, *The Principles of Harmony and Contrast of Colors*, 48.

Both Owen Jones and Christopher Dresser were familiar with these principles. In *The Grammar of Ornament*, Jones states, "No composition can ever be perfect in which any one of the three primary colours is wanting, either in its natural state or in combination." He went on to credit Chevreul's law of simultaneous contrast: "When two tones of the same colour are juxtaposed, the light colour will appear lighter, and the dark colour darker."[9] Dresser, in his *Principles of Decorative Design,* wrote, "No one colour can be viewed by the eye without another being created. Thus, if red is viewed, the eye creates for itself green, and this green is cast upon whatever is near."[10] Chevreul's book had a dramatic effect on French artists searching for different ways of expression—romanticist, impressionist, and cubist—in the nineteenth and early twentieth centuries, and, in his later years, he published a new book incorporating advances in color theory.

Color and Form

When the Bauhaus workshops were established in 1919, the Swiss artist Johannes Itten put together an introductory course on color and form. Itten was familiar with the works of Goethe and Chevreul and added his own theories and research on simultaneous contrast and color harmony. He applied lessons on color and form to the study of works of fine art from antiquity to the twentieth century. As a teacher of painting before and after leaving the Bauhaus, Itten believed creative works were a combination of intuition, education, and observance of nature. He characterized artists according to their three different approaches to color: those who followed the examples of teachers or others; those who painted according to their own inclination; and those with a "universalist" approach, who looked at each situation differently. Itten wrote that design education, rather than being restrictive and inhibiting, could "liberate from indecision."[11]

Itten admired Chinese ceramics, Roman mosaics, medieval stained glass, and neo-impressionist painting. Itten realized the dual nature of color as both visual and emotional; he understood its harmonic relationships to music, its mysterious glow when combined with glass and light; and he wrote, "Colors must have a mystical capacity for spiritual expression, without being tied to objects."[12] Most importantly, Itten pointed out that a color cannot be judged in isolation; when combined with other colors, as it usually is, it takes on an entirely different personality; he gave as examples the "subdued" combination of yellow with pink, in contrast with the "aggressive luminosity" of yellow and black.[13]

Itten delved into the psychological as well as the aesthetic aspects of color in class exercises in which students were asked to do visual "subjective color" essays as a means of self-analysis in the preference of certain colors, before going on to a more intellectu-

9. Owen Jones, *The Grammar of Ornament*, 26. Propositions 23 and 24.

10. Christopher Dresser, *The Principles of Victorian Decorative Design*, 32.

11. Johannes Itten, *The Art of Color*, 12, 30.

12. Johannes Itten, *The Elements of Color*, 6.

13. Johannes Itten, *The Art of Color*, 133.

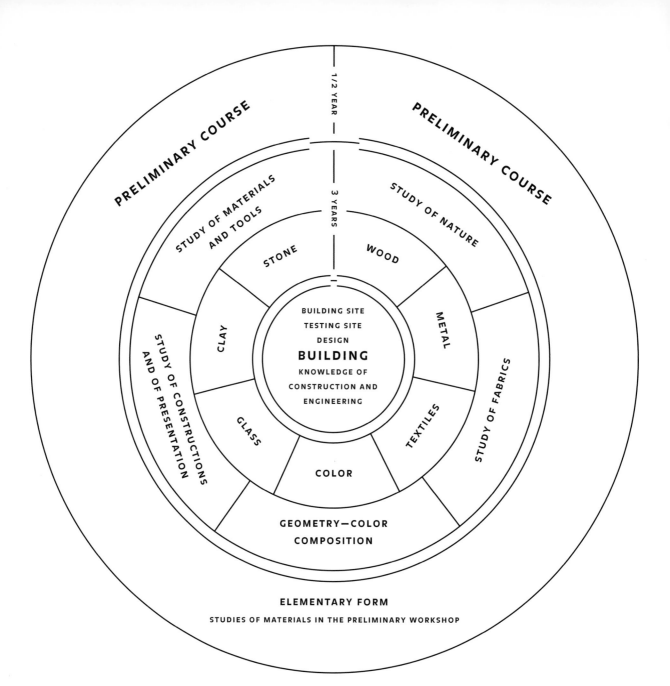

PRELIMINARY COURSE

PRELIMINARY COURSE

1/2 YEAR

3 YEARS

STUDY OF MATERIALS AND TOOLS

STUDY OF NATURE

STUDY OF CONSTRUCTIONS AND OF PRESENTATION

STUDY OF FABRICS

STONE

WOOD

CLAY

METAL

GLASS

TEXTILES

COLOR

BUILDING SITE
TESTING SITE
DESIGN
BUILDING
KNOWLEDGE OF
CONSTRUCTION AND
ENGINEERING

GEOMETRY—COLOR
COMPOSITION

ELEMENTARY FORM
STUDIES OF MATERIALS IN THE PRELIMINARY WORKSHOP

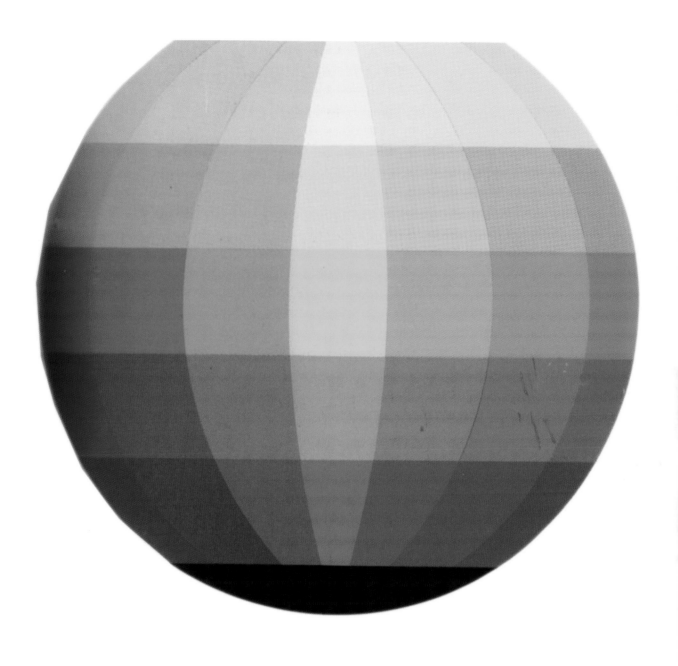

Opposite: The chart outlines the three-year program at the Bauhaus, whose workshops combined theoretical study and practical application. **Above:** Johannes Itten developed a sphere showing colors moving from white and tints at the north pole, to full chroma at the equator, to shades and black at the south pole. Colors are neutralized to gray at the core. He also flattened the sphere to form a twelve-point star showing how colors move from white to tints to full chroma, then taper off into darker, neutralized values.

ally objective level. To a student who intended to become a furniture designer, Itten suggested that the choice of colors showed a strong preference for building materials such as metal and glass; the student went on to design furniture not only in wood but in metal, and later went on to become an architect. The lessons were used not only to have students gain self-understanding but also to point out the need for a professional viewpoint. In his words, "Decorators and designers sometimes tend to be guided by their own subjective color propensities. This may lead to misunderstandings and disputes, where one subjective judgment collides with another. For the solution of many problems, however, there are objective considerations that outweigh subjective preferences."[14]

Itten designed a twelve-color wheel based on the artist's pigment mixtures of primaries, secondaries, and tertiaries, using clearly identifiable primaries so that "a person with normal vision can identify a red that is neither bluish, nor yellowish."[15] The secondaries, he cautioned, had to be mixed as carefully, so as not to favor any of the primaries in the mixture, e.g., the orange must not look too red or yellow. The circle included tertiaries, a mixture of a primary with its neighboring secondary color. He felt any further mixture beyond the twelve was impractical, and artists were advised to consult the circle often as a guide to objective color selection, which is practical advice to this day. Itten continued with Chevreul's studies of simultaneous contrast and after-image. In further experiments, he placed gray squares on bright background colors to show how the eye changes the gray to take on the complement of the background color, while the background color becomes less vibrant because of eye fatigue.

Building on Chevreul's experiments with different proportions of yarns in complementary colors, Itten developed examples to show how equal proportions of two complementary colors change character when one is reduced; for example, with red and green squares, when the amount of red area is greatly reduced, the red remains vibrant, strengthened by the after-image of its complement. Examples like this take on an added dimension of texture, shade, and shadow when they are seen in nature, such as small red berries on a green holly bush.

Itten noted both Goethe's and Chevreul's observations on contrast of colors and made them part of his course by demonstrating how these principles of color and form were used in great paintings over the centuries. The seven principles, in Itten's terminology, were:

---

14. Ibid, 25, 28, 32.
15. Ibid, 34.

1. Contrast of hue–exemplified by works of art based on pure colors found in medieval stained glass, illuminated manuscripts, and the work of renowned Renaissance and modern artists, as well as the more primitive and provincial arts.

2. Light-dark–shows fewer colors, but the colors are heightened by the contrast of light and dark.

3. Cold-warm–contrast used, for example, in the "ice blue" and red of the twelfth-century stained-glass window of the Virgin at Chartres.

4. Complementary contrast—makes use of several tonal and chromatic values of two complementary colors.

5. Simultaneous contrast—a mixture of near-complementary colors, as in Itten's example of an eleventh-century manuscript, which create visual tension.

6. Contrast of saturation—contrasts brilliant pigments with light and dark, and also shows how the contrast of black, white, or gray next to a color heightens its luster.

7. Contrast of extension—more accurately described as contrast of proportion, which deals with the ratio of small and large amounts of different colors.[16]

Another teacher in the basic design course at the Bauhaus was Josef Albers, who enrolled as a student and went on to become technical master of the stained-glass workshop, while the artist Paul Klee was its form master. Albers later became director of the furniture workshop. After emigrating to America, Albers taught at Yale, and his book *Interaction of Color* was the result of experimental studies conducted with students.

Albers compared the wavelengths of color to musical scales in his belief that, just as notes are connected to each other in harmony, colors as we normally see them are connected to other colors and subject to what he called "changing conditions." The focus of his color course was "the interaction of color; that is, seeing what happens between colors."[17] Instead of using yarns or mixed pigments, Albers had students work

16. Ibid, 36, 37, 58, 59, 68, 69, 80, 81, 90, 91, 98, 100, 108, 109.
17. Josef Albers, *Interaction of Color*, 5.

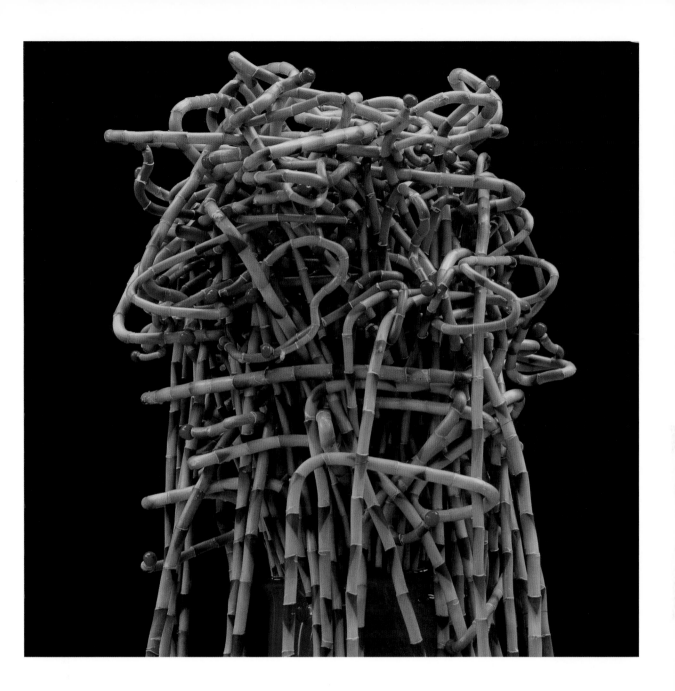

Itten's "contrast of proportion" can be seen in these examples, which use the complementary colors of red and green. In the squares of equal proportion (opposite), the colors compete with each other and vibrate between bright and dull, causing discomfort to the eye. When proportions are changed, the prominent green background projects an after-image of red on the small red squares, making them appear brighter. This contrast can be seen in nature, for example, in a green holly bush with small red berries or in this example (above) from floral designer Daniel Ost's *Leafing Through Flowers,* which shows a contemporary interpretation.

with scraps of paper in a wide array of colors, ranging from light to dark and in varying intensities, because he believed that this method gave a wider range of samples to choose from and enabled them to observe emerging visual phenomena more quickly.

His exercises showed how small chips of the same color placed on larger backgrounds of different colors could change the small samples in varying degrees of both color and intensity. A remarkable example was used on the book's cover, where a single red ocher strip changes from light to dark when its opposite ends are seen against warm and cool colors of different values.

He also demonstrated "middle mixtures" by placing a single color in graded steps ranging from light to dark; where the lighter sample was adjacent to the darker one, its edge looked lighter than the rest of the sample, and the edge of the darker sample looked darker to create a "fluting effect," which he compared to the channels on a Doric column.[18]

In his studies of the change that occurs when colors are juxtaposed, Albers concluded that the assignment of "warm" or "cool" to colors was not always definitive, due to their placement not only with other colors but also with neutrals. He also stated that they were subject to personal interpretation, saying, "there are also warm blues and cool reds possible within their own hues."[19]

Classification of Color

The study of color theories continued to play an equally important role in art and science, from the artist or designer to the rapidly expanding manufacturing industries, including the home furnishings industry—which, in the early twentieth century, felt a need for a system of standardization and classification of color. A meeting in the United States in 1905 between an American artist, Albert Munsell, and a German chemist, Wilhelm Ostwald, was the stimulus for the development of two of the most useful color systems for both the artist and industry in the twentieth century. Ostwald, an amateur painter who four years later was to receive the Nobel Prize in chemistry, was invited to lecture at the Massachusetts Institute of Technology. He held discussions on color theory with Munsell, who had just written *A Color Notation* based on the 1810 color sphere of the German painter Philipp Otto Runge and was trying to solve the problem of identifying colors solely by name. The meeting turned Ostwald to a new career—the challenge of developing a systematic approach to the study of color.

Taking his direction from the late nineteenth-century theories of German psychologist Ewald Hering, whose perceptual approach was based on the four psychological primaries of red, yellow, blue, and green, Ostwald created a system of triangles based

The warm tones of candlelight dramatically illuminate this painting, *The Penitent Magdalen,* by French artist Georges de La Tour. Mirrors were commonly placed near candelabra to reflect more light into the room.

18. Ibid, *37, 38.*
19. Ibid, *59, 60.*

on white, black, and pure color, grading their values between light and dark. His studies were used in color classes at the Bauhaus, and he also worked with the paint industries in Germany to develop a logical order for the classification of colors in their multiple gradations. His system classified colors in two ways: "achromatic," ranging from white through the entire range of clear grays to black; and "chromatic," using the four psychological primaries based on perception—red, yellow, green, and blue—with the entire range of combined colors between them.[20] However, he echoed the centuries-old philosophy of Aristotle and Leonardo in considering white and black (as well as grays) as color, even after labeling them "achromatic."

Ostwald's gray scale was arranged in a linear manner between white and black. Mixing black and white to form gray, he proceeded to further subdivide this mixture in a mathematical progression to obtain distinct visual steps in a scale of grays from white to black. He concluded that equal visual progression differed from numerical progression in determining a gray that looked midway between black and white; visually, there were many more steps from white to medium gray than there were from medium gray to black.

In typical methodical manner, Ostwald arranged red, yellow, green, and blue in a circle by mixing each pure color with its adjacent color and further subdividing these mixtures until one color merged into the other; in other words, clear yellow gradually transitioned in almost invisible divisions through orange into red. He estimated that this process of division could theoretically yield about 300 colors, but he narrowed these down to twenty-four.

Ostwald defines complementary colors as those that will mix optically to clear gray. His wheel of eight "principal colors" shows the complements of yellow and ultramarine blue, red and sea green, purple and leaf green, and turquoise blue and orange. When these were expanded in equidistant steps to a twenty-four-color wheel, there was a larger proportion of greens, ranging from yellow- to blue-greens.

Although gray can only be changed from light to dark, Faber Birren, in his book, *Principles of Color*, illustrated how Ostwald's system of connecting black to white to pure color in triangular form could be plotted in many directions to produce harmonious color combinations; for example, white and black form gray; black mixed with a pure color yields a rich, dark shade; or pure color mixed with white achieves a clear tint. A mixture of white, black, and color produces a "tone," and variations could be achieved by mixing a tint with black, a color with gray, or white with a shade, producing harmonious combinations of white-tone-shade, tint-tone-black, color-tone-gray, or numerous others. Birren compared these harmonious sequences of color with works of great

20. Wilhelm Ostwald, *The Color Primer*, 17, 18.

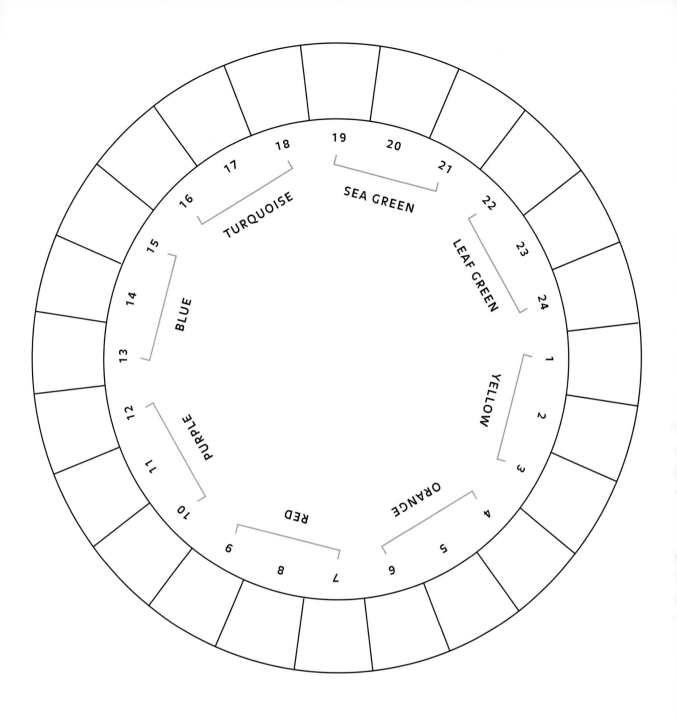

The Ostwald color circle shows a predominance of greens, from yellow to blue greens.

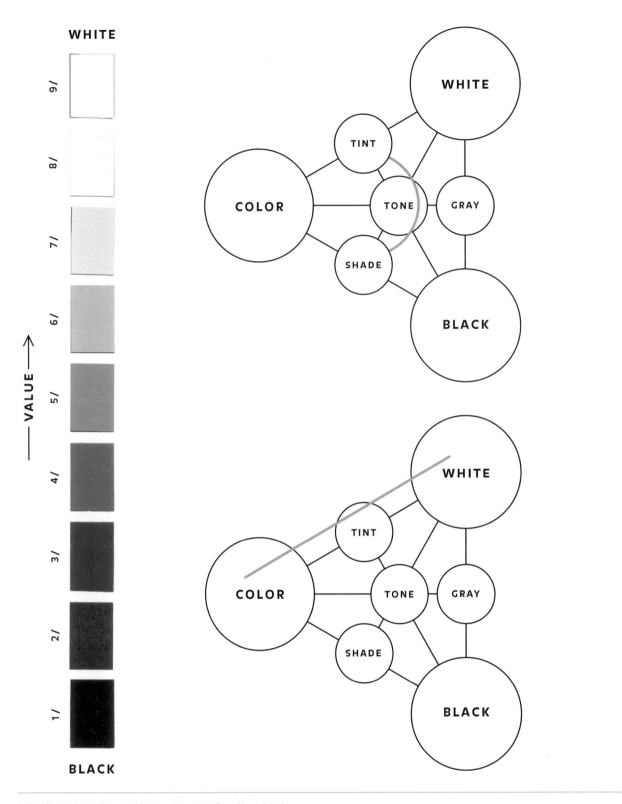

WHITE

9/

8/

7/

6/

5/

4/

3/

2/

1/

BLACK

VALUE →

TINT

COLOR

WHITE

TONE

GRAY

SHADE

BLACK

COLOR

WHITE

TINT

TONE

GRAY

SHADE

BLACK

Left: Albert Munsell's scale of gray values range from No. 1, black,
through steps of grays to white as No. 10.
Right: Ostwald's color triangle was adapted by Faber Birren into color
paths of harmony that could be taken in any direction.

artists. Harmony for Rembrandt took the path of pure color to shade to black; the luminous colors of J.M.W. Turner were the combination of tint, tones, and grays; and, in a more contemporary direction, Mondrian's pure primary colors were juxtaposed with black, white, and gray.

As a teacher as well as an artist, Albert Munsell realized that verbal descriptions or comparisons to fruit, flowers, or gems were inadequate in naming colors; he preferred a comparison of color to notes on a musical scale. Expanding on his *Color Notation*, his *Atlas of the Munsell Color System* in 1915 provided a means to organize colors into a coherent language of color chips, arranged in numerical scale, classifying them by hue, value, and chroma.

Munsell made the distinction between "hue," which defined the color family, such as red, and "color" which could be a range of tonal and chromatic values of the red. He selected the four psychological primaries—red, yellow, green, and blue—plus purple, as the basic hues, which could be further combined into yellow-red, green-yellow, blue-green, purple-blue, and red-purple, for a ten-"hue" or ten-color wheel, which enabled further precise divisions based on a decimal system. Black, white, and gray, to him having no color, were set apart in a neutral category. In addition to hue, "value" represented the lightness or darkness of a color, from tints to shades, and "chroma," a color's intensity or weakening as it approached gray. Tonal and chromatic values were separate, because a light or dark color could be bright or become less intense in steps as it neutralized to gray.

Instead of using the twelve-color wheel based on the painter's palette of primaries, secondaries, and tertiaries, where red falls opposite green as its complement, Munsell organized his circle based on James Clerk Maxwell's scientific research on visual perception and after-image, for, in Munsell's ten-hue circle, blue-green falls opposite red as its complement. His "color tree" was a way of illustrating dimension, with the central core or trunk having black at value level 1 at its base and white at the top, reaching value level 9, with graded grays in between. Branches of different colors reach out in varied lengths according to their chromatic intensity. Yellow, being light, would be at value level 8 (vertically), and its limb would stretch horizontally to a chromatic intensity of twelve; a pure red pigment, being darker, would be at value level 5 but reach a higher chromatic intensity of fourteen.

Munsell was conservative in his approach to color harmony. He believed in using a range of light to dark values but with the middle range of five as the anchor. In chromatic colors as well, the middle range was preferred. In defining the "color paths" through his "color sphere"—which we now refer to as monochromatic, analogous

The color tree of Albert Munsell. A graded scale of grays from white
to black forms the trunk, while branches of color from neutral to pure
chroma fan out in branches.

complementary, or split complementary schemes, among others—he asserted that stronger colors should not overpower weaker ones and that using larger proportions of the weaker colors would achieve balance. Although changing tastes may have disproved some of these theories and his harmonic schemes are formula oriented, his focus on the distribution of color in a range of tonal and chromatic values is still valid in its application to interiors.

Many of the principles of color based on the experiments of theorists on a small scale in textiles or art can be applied on a larger scale to interiors. Chevreul and Albers demonstrated the capricious nature of colors, changing before our very eyes by simply standing next to one another or by our moving farther away. Itten demonstrated that inspiration as well as greater freedom could be achieved by being objective rather than purely subjective. Color can expand or contract, advance or recede, appear warm or cool. The eye, which adjusts to changes of light, changes the colors we see. The rules of harmony set forth by the theorists can act as a guide, but, as each situation is different, there are no universal formulas, and the designer must take on the role of the artist.

3

THE COLORANTS—paints, pigments, and dyes—that we readily take for granted today had their origin in prehistoric times. In early civilizations, the earth's clays were used to make pottery vessels and figures of animals and humans. Weaving is also an ancient craft, and although textiles are not as durable as clay, some examples of fine linens and cottons have been uncovered in Egyptian tombs, preserved by the dry climate.

The earliest known dyes came from plant sources—madder for red, weld for yellow, and woad or indigo for blue. In what is now Turkey, textile fragments of wool dyed with these colors date back to about 6,000 BC[1] Other natural sources of dyes—animal, vegetable, and mineral—later expanded the limited palette. Their extraction was often difficult, but the resulting pigments and dyes imitated nature in their brilliance, and the rarest were highly prized.

Dyes and pigments derived from natural sources are organic—from insects, animals, plants, and trees—or inorganic—from clays and minerals. These colorants can impart color to a yarn, textile, or surface. Dyes are colorants that are completely soluble in the medium, or liquid, with which they are mixed and completely penetrate the material being colored. Pigments, which are used to make paints, are finely ground colored powders that remain suspended and insoluble when combined with a binder or vehicle such as animal fat, plant gum, oil, egg white or yolk, or honey. These binders become an adhesive to join the particles so they can be spread on a surface to harden; they can also be thinned with water or other liquids.

The earth is abundant in iron oxides that supplied the colors in prehistoric caves. Red and yellow ochers were the most commonly used, along with white clay and black manganese oxide or charred bones for black. Minerals were processed into pigment form by grinding and washing, which separated sand from the colored clay, and then dried and pulverized before being mixed with a binder. To increase the variety of colors, organic animal and vegetable dyes were added to white chalklike powdered minerals such as calcite or clay to create insoluble pigments called lakes.

Pigments

Although the earth is generous with red and yellow pigments, it is frugal in its supply of minerals for blues and greens. The Egyptians used lapis lazuli, the rare semiprecious gemstone from Afghanistan, which was powdered to produce ultramarine (meaning "beyond the sea") blue. They made up for the shortage of this source by producing other blues, and greens, from the copper-based minerals azurite and malachite. They used colors for glass and glazes, as well as in wall paintings.

Pigments and Dyes

The Egyptian arts were passed along to Crete, where the Minoans decorated the walls of the Palace of Knossos with fresco (meaning "fresh" in Italian), the technique of painting on wet plaster. In one scene, a crocus gatherer is shown harvesting the flower whose pistils yield the yellow-orange saffron color.

During the Middle Ages, earth pigments took on the names of cities in Italy where they were found in abundance. Raw sienna, named after the Tuscan city of Siena, is dark yellow, but turns a reddish brown when heated or "burnt"; umber (meaning "shade") from the hilly central region of Umbria, is a dark brown (because of its higher manganese content) that is commonly burnt as well. For their frescoes the Romans used red and yellow ochers and green earth, or terre verte, for foliage. Red madder lake was also used, but the wealthiest Romans used cinnabar instead of ocher for red. A sulfide of mercury mined at Almaden, Spain, cinnabar provided the most brilliant red, a color now known as vermilion.

Fresco painting became a major art in Renaissance Italy. It was a relatively inexpensive way to decorate large wall surfaces, and the results were durable, but it required a great deal of skill. In fresco painting, color was applied to plaster walls in two ways: in *buon fresco*, or true fresco, dry pigment mixed with water was applied to wet plaster, where it permanently bonded with the lime in the plaster, which acted as a binder; in *fresco secco* (meaning "dry fresco"), the pigment was mixed with an adhesive binder and applied to dry plaster.

Wet plaster was an unforgiving medium—that is, the paint, once applied, was there to stay; corrections were impossible without removing and redoing the plaster. A full-scale drawing was first made on the wall, and the wet plaster was then applied in sections that could be worked in a day from the top down. A color could be affected by applying it to plaster that was too wet or dry. Very small details were added after the plaster dried, using pigment mixed with an egg yolk or other binder.

Some of the finest examples of *buon fresco* are seen in the fourteenth-century works of Giotto at the Scrovegni Chapel at Padua, the fifteenth-century works of Masaccio at the Brancacci Chapel in Florence, and the sixteenth-century Palladian villas near Venice.

Dyes

The brilliance and luminosity of colors had special appeal to the ancients; gold and red were symbols of the sun and light, and red was centered between light and dark. Purple is not quite as vibrant as red and appears sparingly in nature, or it can be obtained by mixing red and blue.[2] As a dye, it was extremely rare and expensive to obtain and, as a result, was valued as highly as gold.

1. Donald Pavey et al., *Colour,* 60.
2. This distinction between purple and violet should be noted. Violet is part of the electromagnetic spectrum of light; purple is obtained from dyes and is not part of the spectrum.

Page 106: Detail of a Flemish manuscript illumination showing dyers at work (pp. 114–15)

Previous spread, left: Malachite, a mineral that when polished has bands ranging from light to emerald to dark green-black, was at one time pulverized and made into inorganic pigment. Its later, more common use, was as a stone for decorative ornaments and tabletops.

Previous spread, right: Lapis lazuli, a semi-precious stone, was pulverized to make ultramarine blue, which was as valuable as gold before the discovery of synthetic pigments.

Above: *The Visitation,* c.1305 by Giotto, The Scrovegni Chapel, Padua. Frescoes that were painted in *buon fresco,* on wet plaster, had to be divided into sections that could be completed before the plaster dried.

Colors in this Fortuny fabric, "Olimpia," after a seventeenth-century
Italian design, capture the opulence of malachite and gold.

Reds were readily available in earth, plants, and berries, but the most brilliant reds and purple dyes came from the animal family: crimson from the kermes insect, and purple, reserved for the emperors of ancient Rome, from a species of Mediterranean sea snail, the murex or "purpura," from which the name is derived. Manufacture of the dye, which is thought to have been closer to a very deep red, may go as far back as 1439 BC when, in the ancient coastal city of Tyre (now in Lebanon), the Phoenicians extracted and processed the "red juice" of the snail, as Goethe called it. They left vast deposits of discarded murex shells in the sea and in hills at Sidon and transported the Tyrian Purple to civilizations along the Mediterranean. Thousands of snails were needed in order to produce a minute quantity of the dye, and a photochemical change added mystery to its appeal. In the process of being exposed to light, the yellowish color turned first to green, then blue-green, and then to red-purple.

The Middle Ages brought not only the dramatic appearance of stained-glass windows but also an accompanying taste for brightly colored, luxurious fabrics. From the twelfth century through the Renaissance, Italy was the leading center for the production of expensive silks and dyes. The supply of murex purple had been depleted, but, in a thriving trade with Asia, indigo, saffron, and kermes were brought to Florence, Venice, and Genoa where, in the hands of skilled dyers, they were turned into exquisite fabrics that supplied the courts of Europe.

Commonly used colorants in the Middle Ages were the madder plant for red, and woad, which was turned into blue dye through a complicated and lengthy process of grinding, drying, and fermentation. Both madder and woad were abundant in Europe, but the colors were unstable. These were improved through dyeing techniques and the use of mordants, chemical compounds that bonded the dye to the fabric. Most plant dyes required mordants to create brighter, more permanent colors, and sources ranged from mineral salts to acidic compounds. A common mordant was alum, a chemical compound of aluminum, sulfate, and potassium. It was in wide use in the fifteenth century, when a sharp increase in the cost of its import caused a temporary panic. This shortage was relieved by the discovery of alum deposits in Italy, on land under papal control. Further imports were then banned, and the mines were leased to the Medici family of Florence, becoming the foundation of their immense wealth.

Alchemists played a significant role in the development of dyes during the Middle Ages. Part magic and part chemistry, alchemy was an ancient art that evolved from metalwork. It was passed down through Arab scholars, influenced by Greek philosophy, and then filtered through Europe in the twelfth century. Through experiments with chemicals and metals, alchemists were absorbed by the seemingly magical transmuta-

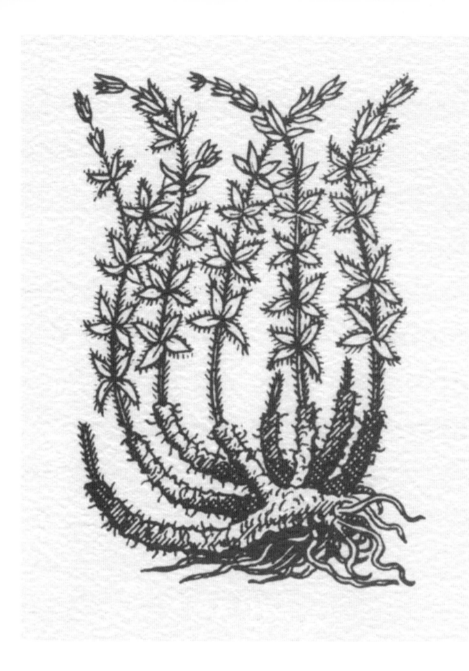

Above: The madder plant, whose roots provided a common source of red dye in the Middle Ages.

Opposite: This scene from a late medieval illuminated manuscript shows Flemish dyers at work.

tion of substances, including the progressive stages of color in some substances and the changes of some materials, like glass, to completely different colors by altering the heating time. Often deceptive, alchemists tried to conceal their formulas in obscure language, which added to their ill-repute. To the alchemist, red symbolized the philosopher's stone, which was believed to hold the key to the formula for transmuting base metals into gold, the most perfect of materials; thus, the fabled stone symbolized the attainment of perfection. Red may also be symbolic, since it was one of the earliest colors produced by combining mercury with sulphur. The resulting color, vermilion, was used as a substitute for cinnabar as far back as the eighth century. The goal of creating gold out of base metals remained elusive, but the experiments of alchemists led to the eventual formation of chemistry as a science.

Indigo, one of the oldest of plant dyes, and one that yields a deep, strong blue, was brought from Asia to Europe by Venetian and Genoese traders. Although more expensive than woad, indigo required no mordant and produced a richer, more durable color with a smaller quantity of dye. Leaves of the subtropical indigo bush were carefully harvested, steeped in water, fermented, and dried before being shipped in blocks. In a surprising transformation, textiles that were green when removed from the colorless liquid in the dye vats turned blue within a short time after exposure to air.

The growing popularity of indigo in the fourteenth century created a conflict with prosperous local woad producers, who prohibited dyers from using the imports. Discovery of the New World and colonization of the West Indies by the Spaniards opened a supply of new varieties of indigo, and its cultivation by slave labor created an even greater threat of a large supply at a lower price, to the point where, in the seventeenth and eighteenth centuries, penalties for its use were imposed in parts of France and Germany. Despite this, indigo was so superior that the bans were eventually removed, and the dye remained the most popular source of blue until the development of synthetic dyes in the nineteenth century.

From antiquity to the Middle Ages, the most vivid and expensive red dyes were derived from kermes, female insects that looked like berries clinging to trees and shrubs, whose extract produced a deep crimson. Imported from the Near East to Genoa and Venice, kermes kept European nobles and cardinals encased in red. In the sixteenth century, Spanish explorers in the Americas discovered a new supply of red dye, which became a treasure as valuable as the spices and Aztec gold they were seeking. The cochineal insect, like the kermes, is a parasite, but one that attaches itself to cactus plants; for centuries it had been a source of red dye for the native Indians of Mexico and Central America. It produced a strong, high quality crimson dye, and the harvesting

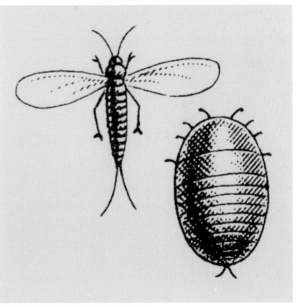

Above: The woad plant, along with indigo, was one of the earliest
known sources of blue dye.

Below: The cochineal insect, an early source of red dye for native
Indians of Mexico and Central America.

COAL TAR DYES.

SPECIMENS OF FABRICS DYED WITH

Simpson, Maule & Nicholson's

COLORS.

Concentrated Regina
Purple.

Concentrated Violet with
a little Roseine.

Phosphine.

Roseine.

Regina Purple.

Violet.

Phosphine.

Printers Roseine.

Regina Purple.

No. 2 Violet.

No. 1 Blue.

Blue.

No. 2 Blue & Violet.

Concentrated Printers
Roseine.

SPECIMENS OF FABRICS DYED WITH

Perkin & Son's Colors.

This chart from an 1862 journal shows samples of colors produced by
the new aniline dyes.

and processing of the cochineal quickly replaced that of kermes to become a major industry for the colonies. The Spanish, in order to protect their source, were secretive about its origin and production and prohibited the export of live insects. Dried insects were sent to Spain for secret processing, and huge orders were shipped to clients such as Louis XIV, who used the color for the decoration of Versailles. The monopoly was eventually broken as cultivation spread to the West Indies and Asia.

Chemistry and Color

Just as the Spanish quest for gold led to equal riches in the discovery of a new source of a valuable dye, the alchemist's search for gold led to the development of new color sources that would virtually eliminate the pigments and dyes of the past. In 1668, an alchemist produced a blue-red that became known under his name as Cassius purple. In 1704, one of the most significant synthetic pigments was made in Berlin by two alchemists, Johann Konrad Dieppel and Diesbach (his full name is unknown), who, in using tainted potassium to mix red, accidentally discovered the deep, intense Prussian blue. Alchemy developed into the discipline of chemistry in the eighteenth century, with precise weights and measurements, and accurate records replacing cryptic formulas. In addition to new dyes, a synthetic alum was produced, and chemists like Chevreul expanded the study of color to include visual interaction and psychological effects.

In 1826, a German chemist distilled a liquid from the indigo plant and called it "aniline," a word that stems from *annil*, the Arabic name for indigo. Aniline was also derived by distilling coal tar, and these discoveries of "synthetic organic" dyes, also called aniline dyes, revolutionized the color industry.

From the mid-nineteenth century, the discovery and development of aniline dyes accelerated rapidly. In 1856, William Henry Perkin, a young English student, in an attempt to synthesize quinine while using coal tar, created the first aniline dye— purple, or mauve, as the French called it. August Wilhelm von Hoffman, Perkin's teacher, in 1858 developed a magenta and other synthetic colors—violet, green, blue, and a bright red that was to replace the more expensive cochineal. The following year, a French chemist synthesized fuchsia, a purplish red named after the flower. In 1868, German chemists were able to synthesize alizarin red, the colorant that came from the madder plant. Up to this time, madder was one of the most widely used dyes, and the acres of land where it had been grown were turned into vineyards to create a different, more palatable red.[3] Woad and indigo would also be displaced when indigo was synthetically produced at the end of the century. Not only was the hand of the craftsman being replaced by the machine in the industrial 1800s, but by the chemist as well.

3. Donald Pavey et al., *Colour*, 88.

Artists' Pigments

Careful recipes for mixing pigments came down from the twelfth-century monk Theophilus, whose treatise on painting gave helpful advice on colors and technique.[4] One formula for making vermilion sounds like an alchemist's brew. It calls for combining ground sulphur with "half as much mercury," sealing it in a flask, setting it to dry, and then heating it until you "hear a noise inside."[5] Mineral-based pigments as well as colored lake were most often used—blues from lapis lazuli or azurite; greens from copper or earth; red, yellow, and black from ochers; mercury-based vermilion, or minium red; and lead white. A notable figure in the move from the medieval to Renaissance attitude toward art was Cennino Cennini, a Florentine painter who wrote the *Libro dell' arte (The Craftsman's Handbook)*, c. 1400. This detailed instructional manual on the preparation of pigments and their application, along with aesthetic advice, was part of Cennini's attempt to raise the role of the painter from artisan to artist.

Paints and Their Use Today

Today, both traditional and synthetic pigments are used in artists' and household paints. In addition to color, important factors in paints include chromatic value or vibrancy, permanence, and toxicity. Either unknowingly or because of cost, some nineteenth-century artists used paints that proved fugitive, fading over time. Other pigments such as vermilion, based on mercury, Naples yellow, on lead, and Paris green, on arsenic, were extremely toxic. Interior paints were also at one time lead-based and toxic, but these have been banned.

Sparkle and luminosity as well as pure, vibrant color have always been valued in pigments and dyes. Interior walls at Pompeii were waxed or polished to an almost mirror finish. Artists prepared canvases with chalk white, or gesso, a form of plaster mixed with an adhesive, to give a base that would not diminish the color. Today, many household paints have pearlized finishes to catch and reflect light like facets on a gem.

Color Mixtures

Looking at porcelains or paintings in museums is an excellent way to develop an understanding of the nuances of color. One of the best ways to train the eye is to actually mix colors using an opaque, water-based paint such as gouache, in order to be able to see the most subtle differences. Following Itten's advice, the color wheel should be used as a guide to help understand how mixtures affect color, for example, that red added to neighboring orange will make the orange look redder.

4. The word "pigment" comes from the Latin *pigmentum*, meaning "to paint." Before merchants took over the preparation of pigments they had to be mixed from raw materials by the artist or assistants and placed in pig bladders for storage. In addition to gold, lapis lazuli was the most costly material; its extraction and the preparation of the brilliant ultramarine blue was complex. It was most often billed separately and used sparingly on only the most important subjects in the painting. Michel Pastoureau, *Blue*, 117; John Gage, *Color and Meaning*, 42; François Delamare and Bernard Guineau, *Colors, The Story of Dyes and Pigments*, 49, 75, 115.

5. Delamare and Guineau, Ibid., 141.

Leaves on the same tree will take on different colors as they are seen in light and shadow. Paints that contain a touch of all colors of the spectrum can take on the same textural depth with the changing light. (*Natural Palettes for Painted Rooms,* 12)

Dark, medium, and light neutral bases.

Adding black to white will create a gray that is dull and lifeless. More interesting grays can be obtained by a mixture of the primaries, or primaries and secondaries, to produce a warmer or cooler gray, which can then be lightened with white. Adding color to white to produce a tint will result in a cool, bluish tint, which can be warmed with a little yellow or orange. Adding colors directly to white may result in a "chalky" white; this can be buffered by first mixing a neutral base with white and a touch of green and burnt sienna or umber, which looks neither red nor green, and then adding the color. Adding black may "extinguish" a color by absorbing its light—it is better to use a darkened mixture of many colors. Using black to darken yellow will turn it green.

There are hundreds of whites and almost as many grays produced by paint manufacturers. Almost all have a hint of color, which may not be obvious when the color is seen alone, but, when it is placed on a chalk-white background or next to a different sample, the color will be readily visible. Blacks can also have undertones of other colors.

When one looks at paint samples, whether a color, a neutral, or an off-white, some will look dull, while others have an appealing liveliness. Color consultants Donald Kaufman and Taffy Dahl believe that every color or neutral should have in its mixture a touch of all colors of the spectrum, rather than the minimal number found in many commercial paints. This subtle mixture simulates the balance found in nature and adds a textural depth to the color, which takes on a different character as the changing light is reflected from the surface. The same is true for mixtures of dyes. The fabric to be dyed is also a factor; a bright red may look garish on a synthetic, yet elegant on silk.

As much as the eye needs the full spectrum of color, it craves neutral areas for relief. Other than black, white, and gray, warmer neutrals are beige and taupe (gray/beige). Although these will have subtle undertones of color, if they have too much color, they may cease to be a neutral. Although neutral means "not decided in color; nearly achromatic," people will sometimes identify a color such as yellow or gold as a neutral rather than as a color.

William Morris, in his use of white at a time when colors in Victorian interiors were dark, may have influenced architects of the modern movement, who eliminated not only ornament from interiors but color as well, relying mostly on pristine white and using color as an accent or in natural materials. Decorators in Morris's time had a very limited range of paints to work with, and white offered a refreshing alternate. Today, however, with paint companies supplying a limitless range of every conceivable color, with skilled designers and an educated public, the most popular choice for walls is still white.

4

THROUGHOUT HISTORY, NATURAL DYES AND PIGMENTS have been removed from the earth and its creatures to color clothing and decorate walls. Nature's color is functional as well as beautiful, giving camouflage to animals and recycling the turning leaves before the onset of winter. The colors of fall are erased by snow, which paints scenes in black and white that invite contemplation by shifting the focus from color to texture, shade, and shadow.

The Asian concept of black-and-white ink painting with tonal variations of gray is carried over to Zen gardens of sand and rocks, in which the monochromatic, raked sand becomes colorless waves in the sea, while rocks form a mini-landscape, and a near-absence of color provides peace and calm. Identical grains of sand in the desert take on a sharp contrast of values from light to dark as they are paved into wave patterns by shifting winds.

Winter scenes bring to mind two techniques of painting: chiaroscuro, the contrast of light and dark; and grisaille, monochromatic painting in gray values that make a surface appear three-dimensional. On the walls of the Scrovegni Chapel in Padua, Giotto painted frescoes in grisaille to portray statues of the Virtues and Vices (see p. 131) in marble niches. Grisaille was also used in making studies for painting, and, in the eighteenth century, in the decoration of interiors as a trompe l'oeil technique on walls and furniture medallions.

The emphasis on color to define form in antiquity was overturned in the Renaissance by Leonardo da Vinci, whose use of chiaroscuro was to change the course of painting. In *A Treatise on Painting*, Leonardo wrote that the "perfection of art comes from the true and natural arrangement of light and shade, or what is called chiaroscuro; thus if a painter dispenses with shadows when they are necessary, he wrongs himself and renders his work despicable to connoisseurs, to win the worthless applause of the vulgar and ignorant, who look only at the brilliance and gaiety of the color in a picture, and care nothing for the relief."[1] He recognized that the contrast of light and dark in a painting could achieve depth and distance and make a flat surface appear three-dimensional. Instead of focusing solely on formal composition, he introduced an emotional and philosophical element in his use of black and white, or light and total darkness.

Leonardo's art reflects his connection with nature in its many moods and motions. Figures in his paintings are often seen against a background of mountains, trees, and water that fade in the distance. He combined chiaroscuro with *sfumato*, a series of subtle tonal variations that added a lifelike softness of form and expression to humans and nature. Although his work was more tonal than heavily colored, Leonardo set forth

Tonal Values and Natural Forms

Page 124: Detail of Albert Bierstadt's *Rocky Mountains* (p. 132).

Previous spread: Nature often clothes animals in the colors of their surroundings as protection against predators, from white polar bears in the arctic to tropical birds that blend in with exotic foliage and flowers. English artist and naturalist Mark Catesby traveled to America to document unknown species of plant and animal life. His portrait of "The Great Hog Fish" from *The Natural History Watercolors from his Journey to Carolina, Florida & the Bahama Islands 1722–1726* illustrates how nature continues its eccentric textures and colors under water.

Opposite: Light and shadow are used to create the texture of water in furious movement during a storm. In this print, the contrast of tonal values—the light waves against darker ones—thrust the ship upward as well as outward toward the viewer, giving a three-dimensional effect on a flat surface. Heliodore-Joseph Pisan, after Gustave Dore, for Samuel Coleridge's *The Rime of the Ancient Mariner*. Gillotage of wood engraving, French 1877. MMA

Above: Chiaroscuro, the contrast of light and dark, is as effectively used in black and white photography as it is by the artist in Zen ink painting, or in pencil or charcoal drawings. The flowing movement of the wood, emphasized by the sharp contrast of light and dark, would be diminished by the distraction of color. *Cypress, Point Lobos, California, 1929.* Edward Weston, American. MMA

Above: *The Annunciation to St. Anne,* fresco by Giotto, The Scrovegni Chapel, Padua.

Below: Johannes Itten's simplified, abstract study of Giotto's fresco *The Annunciation to St. Anne.* Itten developed exercises to study the contrast effects of chiaroscuro, or light and dark. In these value analyses of paintings, his students were better able to understand their geometric composition and subsequent expression.

Opposite, above: Grisaille paintings by Giotto of the Virtues and Vices take on the appearance of marble, shown here in the Scrovegni Chapel, where Fortitude stands opposite Inconstancy.

Opposite, below: Grisaille painting on this *kas,* or cabinet, gives it the sculptured, three-dimensional look of carving. The Hewlett Room, Woodbury, New York, 1740–60, The Metropolitan Museum of Art.

Above: Albert Bierstadt creates receding layers of depth by imitating
the variation of light and shadow in nature. Dark colors in the
foreground fade into the distance. The contrast calls attention to the
light waterfall and ties it into the notion of melting snow in the
distance. *Rocky Mountains,* 1863.

Below: The contrast of very light and dark, in addition to creating a
sense of depth, supports both rigid and flowing geometric forms in the
1891 lithograph, *Le Jour* by Odilon Redon. The light exterior evokes a
feeling of freedom and movement, while the dark interior appears
immovable and oppressive.

principles later documented by nineteenth-century theorists, for example, that light against dark will make the light appear lighter and the dark darker; and that colors are affected by surrounding colors. He observed the gradations of tonal values that occur in nature, and noted that colors were reflected in shadows, and that highlights could be achieved with pure, strong colors.

The invention of photography in the nineteenth century introduced an entirely new version of black and white. Artists' portraits or sketches of monuments on the grand tour were replaced with black-and-white photographic images. Instead of Adam's drawings of Spalato or Napoleon's entourage of artists recording the monuments of Egypt, archeological discoveries and exotic places and peoples rarely seen by Europeans were captured on film. Images could be taken at different times of day, with the changing light providing different moods with shadows, either softly blurred or with brutally sharp edges. Early black-and-white movies and television continued the drama without the distraction of color, much as radio, without pictorial images, forced the listener to use his or her imagination. Photography began to replace painting in bringing realistic outdoor scenes indoors, just as picture windows would later begin to replace landscape paintings. The discipline of uniting exterior with interior in terms of color, value, and texture became a new challenge.

It is hard to imagine a completely solid color in nature. A violet, for example, may have a range of light, medium, and dark colors—very dark violet where the semitransparent petals overlap, and highlights and shadow caused by curvature of the petals. These changes in tonal value create a sense of texture. What at first glance looks like a simple color has an underlying complexity when viewed up close.

In the ancient world, structural and decorative details in architecture were often inspired by tree and plant forms, which gracefully connected columns and capitals and brought massive buildings down to human scale through texture, shade, and shadow. Foliage in stone created texture that was animated by changing light and shadows, as leaves on a tree create a texture of values and layered colors. Delicate arabesques lightened the heavy black walls at Boscotrecase as radiating branches lighten the bulk of a large tree. Naturalistic forms were also used indoors as decorative elements on columns and moldings, and then filtered down to furniture, carpets, and accessories.

Nature's colors are the first impact of a garden. History records the description of a sixth-century Persian carpet that was woven to represent a colorful garden divided by streams. The intent was to capture spring all year, with brightly contrasting colors of red, yellow, blue, and white. Abstract floral and geometric patterns, and deliberate imperfections were part of the garden carpet's charm. Chevreul, who was not fond of

1. Faber Birren, *Color and Human Response*, 54. From "A Treatise on Painting," Leonardo da Vinci.

analogous combinations, noted that the combination of red and violet found in the sweet pea looked better when separated by white. Despite the mixture of all colors crowded together in a garden, Christopher Dresser noted, "When viewed from a distance the effect is soft and rich, and full and varied . . . . This is nature's colouring."[2]

The connection of nature with interiors took on a new look at the start of the twentieth century. Although preliminary exploration of the Palace of Knossos in Crete had begun in 1878, it was not until 1900 that English archaeologists began a six-year excavation. To their surprise, the ancient ruins turned out to be unexpectedly "modern" in their resemblance to the Art Nouveau style already firmly in place before their excavation work began.[3] Frescoes of birds and stylized vegetation on the palace walls looked strikingly similar to wallpaper designs of the day, while frescoes of women with curling hair (see pp. 138–39) that resembled flowing vines showed a remarkable resemblance to the women in Art Nouveau posters.[4] These sinuous forms were carried into the first Art Nouveau interior by Victor Horta at the Tassel House (1893–95) in Brussels where, in the stair hall, ironwork, murals, stained glass, marble, and mosaic, they were woven together in natural, curving forms to reinforce the concept of circulation.

In Europe in the late eighteenth and early nineteenth centuries, there was great interest in non-European styles: Egyptian, Moorish, and Oriental, among others. In England, artists and writers such as James McNeill Whistler and Oscar Wilde were part of an Aesthetic Movement, which sought to beautify interiors in a more lavish way than the more reserved Arts & Crafts. As an eccentric branch of the Art Nouveau movement, their quest was for "art for art's sake." One of the best examples of an Aesthetic Movement interior is the Peacock Room by Whistler, housed at the Freer Gallery of Art in Washington, D.C. Inspired by Japanese art, Whistler designed the room in London for Frederick Leyland in 1876–77. Magnificent golden peacocks appear to dance on the walls, and the ceiling is decorated with a feather pattern.

The colors of the peacock have held fascination since antiquity, through the combination of their jewellike colors—emerald, sapphire, gold and an elusive purple—and their iridescence, caused by the refraction of light on the structure of their feathers. A favorite motif in the glassware of American painter and designer Louis Comfort Tiffany was the peacock feather; Tiffany is most associated with Favrile glass, a name derived from an Old English word roughly meaning "handcrafted." He was inspired by ancient glass and its imperfections, as well as the luster that was caused by corrosion, and he was able to achieve the same effect on his Favrile glass through the use of metallic fumes in the work process. Tiffany looked to the natural world for his themes of flowers, plants, and feathers. His exotic interiors, glassware, lamps, and jewelry were also

2. Christopher Dresser, *Principles of Victorian Decorative Design*, 46.

3. Alexandre Farnoux, *Knossos, Searching for the Legendary Palace of King Minos*, 108.

4. Ibid, 104, 105, 107.

Previous spread: The typical tonal values of nature—light sky, medium foliage, and dark earth—are dramatically displaced in this photo of a storm. The sharp contrast of black and white emphasizes the contour of the landscape, while gray shadows give the clouds a filmy defense against the overbearing sky. *Lake George: Dark Hills in Profile against Sky.* Alfred Stieglitz (1864–1946).

Opposite: The Tassel House, Brussels (1892–93). Tendrils wend their way over all surfaces of this hall, from the mosaic floor pattern to the painted wall mural and up the wrought-iron stairway.

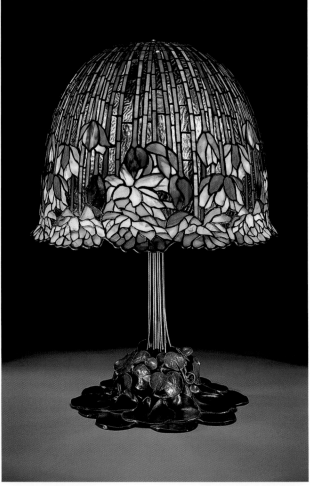

inspired by his travels, on which he was captivated by the colors—those of Moorish and Islamic architecture in North Africa; of the Early Christian mosaics in Ravenna, Italy; of the stained-glass windows at Chartres.

Colors are also best seen in the works of glassware designers such as Emile Gallé, whose work was admired by Tiffany on an 1889 Paris visit. Gallé studied, in addition to art and philosophy, zoology and botany, and he was highly influenced by the Japanese arts. He believed the duty of the artist was not to copy forms but to convey them in a spiritual sense in order to capture "the essence of what he sees and experiences."[5] Gallé's vases reflect the beauty he perceived in all of nature, in dragonflies and other insects, in flowers, and in the uniqueness of varied plant forms.

Scottish architect and designer Charles Rennie Mackintosh, equally a lover of natural forms, was also influenced by Japanese art and architecture. He took a minimalist approach, combined with various medieval styles and a classical clarity of form to create uniquely individual buildings. In the interiors, he played the geometry of a grid against the ornamental motif of an abstracted rose; to natural oak furniture he added decorative inserts of tile, mosaic, glass, and metal; and with dark woods and white, he combined the soft colors of rose pink, green, blue, and violet. His elongated chairs made of dark oak or stained ash became vertical, sculptural forms against contrasting white walls.

A subtle theme in the variation of a rose and trellis grid was woven through the interior of one of Mackintosh's finest residential projects, Hill House in Helensburgh, Scotland (1902–04). In the entrance hall, dark wall panels were inset with slender, rose-colored tiles, and a grid pattern was carried from carpet border to doors to windows. In the drawing room, which overlooks a garden, the light walls were covered with a stenciled rose and trellis pattern, which was carried into the lighting. The ceiling was painted black, and a subtle grid was added to the carpet. Abstract rose insets that end in a grid on the all-white bedroom's wardrobe closets draw the eye upward, and the grid theme is repeated in the tall black chairs.

In America in the early twentieth century, Frank Lloyd Wright built his Midwestern prairie houses, which spread horizontally instead of vertically to conform to the flat plains in a new style he described as "planted" on American soil.[6] In his book, *The Natural House*, Wright stated that he saw walls as a cave imprisoning the occupants, and he strived to open up boxlike rooms through the "miracle" of glass, to make the sky part of the interior. He further freed the occupants by removing interior walls or by treating them as screens to promote indoor circulation and, where possible, he eliminated doors. In a contrast with this outward expansion, the fireplace, an ancient symbol

Previous spread: *Ladies in Blue* fresco from the Palace of Knossos (Herakleion Museum). The flowing curls of the ladies' coiffures presage the winding tendril motifs of the Art Nouveau movement, which can be seen in the stair hall of the Tassel House (p. 137).
Opposite, above: The Peacock Room, 1876–77, James McNeill Whistler, Freer Gallery of Art, Washington, DC.
Opposite, below left: Louis Comfort Tiffany's Favrile glass vases capture the iridescence of the peacock's feathers. The Metropolitan Museum of Art, Tiffany Glass & Decorating Company Vase, 1893–96.
Opposite, below right: Other favorite natural motifs of Louis Comfort Tiffany were flowers, leaves, and vines. Soft warm and cool colors are seen in this water lily lamp of leaded Favrile glass set on a bronze base (1904–15).

5. Gabriele Fahr-Becker, *Art Nouveau*, 114, 382: "Ecrits pour l'Art," 1884–1889, Emile Gallé.
6. Frank Lloyd Wright, *The Natural House*, 106. "Planted" is used in the sense of an organic extension of the land, not planted in the soil, as Wright eliminated the basement.

Above: The Frank Lloyd Wright Room, Wayzata, Minnesota 1912–14. The Metropolitan Museum of Art. The broad, horizontal oak band that divides the upper and lower walls of this room appear to exert a downward pressure to set it firmly on the ground. Rather than break the wall plane with double-hung windows, Wright used casement and added clerestory windows above to admit more light and sky. However, he interrupted the view by breaking the windows into segments with leaded glass designs. Wright designed total interiors, including furniture and lighting. Exterior materials of wood and brick were brought indoors in their natural finish, and the textured plaster walls are a natural ocher color.

of warmth and comfort, was centered inward. Wright believed materials should be what they are, "glass is used as glass, stone as stone, wood as wood." and brought outdoor materials of wood, brick, and stone indoors.[7]

In true organic fashion, interior elements in Wright's houses were connected: furniture was set into walls, lights into the ceiling, and fireplaces interlocked with bookcases, which connected to seating. Walls, floor, ceiling, furniture, and textiles were all woven together. Instead of applied ornament, Wright's focus was on light and the texture and color of materials. Woods carried the warm tones of orange, yellow, and brown; brick, the terra-cotta colors; stained-glass windows, the brighter reds, blues, and greens; and textiles, the more subtle tones of these colors. Glass was often given texture by breaking it down into smaller segments, and Wright fashioned windows to play with exterior views in unique ways—by placing a clear center within a border of leaded patterned glass,[8] or by cutting abstract animal shapes in a paneled wall.[9] Furniture was related to walls in its heavy architectural look, and by being footed in the floor like a hard-to-move rock. Having little use for what he considered the antiquated textiles of William Morris, Wright designed his own fabrics in textured, solid colors or small, geometric patterns, as well as furniture, carpets, and lamps. In doing so, he carried into the twentieth century the tradition of the seventeenth- and eighteenth-century architects, for whom architecture and interior decoration were part of a cohesive whole under their direction.

Opposite, below: The master bedroom at Hill House. The abstract rose motif on a white background softens the geometry of the wardrobe cabinet and adds a touch of color to which the eye is immediately drawn, like to a spotlight on a stage. The square grid of the tall-back chair provides a visual connection to the elongated grid on the cabinet.

7. Ibid, 123.

8. Winslow House, River Forest, IL. Dining Room/Conservatory. Frank Lloyd Wright Trust.

9. Pope-Leighey House, Falls Church, VA.

3

THE
APPLICATION
OF
COLOR
TO
INTERIORS

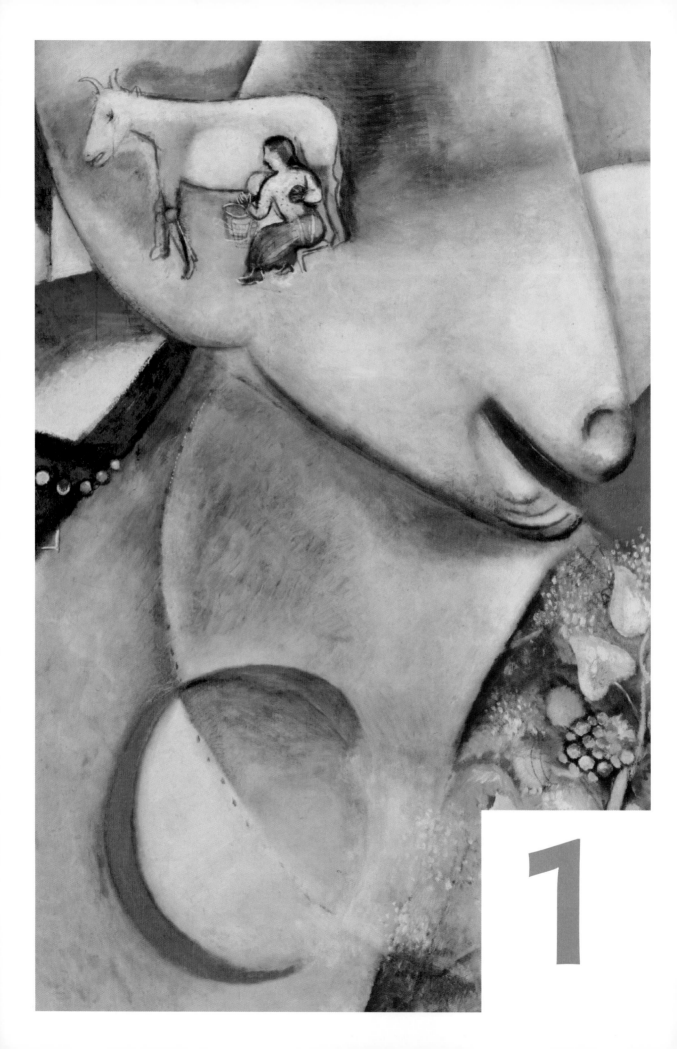

WHILE FRANK LLOYD WRIGHT WAS APPLYING ORGANIC CONCEPTS to Midwestern architecture, a collaboration between Boston architect Ogden Codman and New York City–born author Edith Wharton produced a book, *The Decoration of Houses* (1897), that would launch the profession of interior design as we know it today.

Wharton lived and traveled in Europe and was deeply impressed by sixteenth-century Italian architecture and its subsequent influence on French and English interiors through the eighteenth century. She appreciated that the architect in these periods was also responsible for the decoration and furnishings, which resulted in a unified interior. *The Decoration of Houses* was primarily a reaction to the "dubious eclecticism" of Victorian interiors, in which the decorator (known at the time as the "upholsterer") was called in to add furnishings and ornament after the architect completed his work, most often with chaotic results. Wharton sought to remedy this by reconnecting architecture with interior decor and by going back to the discipline of classical proportions, not to copy, but to creatively reinterpret tradition.

Wharton believed rooms should be furnished for their intended use and the comfort of the occupants, while honoring the organic concept that "Structure conditions ornament, not ornament structure."[1] To her, a well-proportioned room could stand on its own without "surface application" of ornament.[2] She believed that period decoration should not be applied to a room whose architectural proportions as well as its voids and solids of windows and door openings were incompatible with that period. When this principle was ignored, the decorator was called in to camouflage the flaws with color or yards of drapery, or to fill in the voids with useless "bric-à-brac."[3]

To Wharton, the first step in decorating a room was to look at three components: the shell—that is, the walls, floor, and ceiling; the room's proportions; and the balance of voids and solids in window and door openings. The second step was a decision on the hierarchy of walls and floor to furniture: was the floor to act as a background for furniture, or were the walls to be a background for furniture and artwork? Or, were floor and walls to be the focus of the room with paneling or pattern, while furniture took a secondary role? Ceilings were likewise to have appropriate proportions in their height and never to be treated as an extension of the walls.

Believing that form was more important than color, and that bad design could not be corrected by the application of either ornament or color, Wharton had distinct views on the use of color. She favored the approach of the Italians, who, for example, used wood inlay in a range of light values on doors to blend harmoniously with the range of values in marble used in the interior, over that of the English, who contrasted mahogany doors with white trim. "Concerning the difficult question of color," she wrote, "it is safe

Architectural Concepts and Artists

Page 146: Detail of *I and the Village*, by Marc Chagall (p. 151).

Above: Ogden Codman worked with Edith Wharton on the decoration of her Park Avenue home. Shown here is a section of the dining room; the marble fireplace is French, c.1895. Wharton disliked wallpaper but admired the scenic frescoes of interiors at Pompeii, which she thought were an ideal wall treatment for smaller rooms.

to say that the fewer the colors used in a room, the more pleasing and restful the result will be. A multiplicity of colors produces the same effect as a number of voices talking at the same time. The voices may not be discordant, but continuous chatter is fatiguing in the long run."[4] Just as too many colors caused confusion, overcrowded rooms made it difficult to appreciate art and furniture, and fine objects were best presented with open space around them. The eye had limits in what it could absorb. Restraint was also needed in scaling art and furniture to rooms. Believing poor design could be corrected only up to a point, her advice was to either rectify it or live with it, as "Half-way remedies are a waste of money and serve to call attention to the defects of the room rather than to conceal them."[5]

Wharton did not oppose the use of ornamentation, but rather advocated its appropriate use instead of haphazard application. In his book on the mélange of traditions that were blended to create the distinctive architecture of Venice, John Ruskin, one of Wharton's sources of inspiration,[6] wrote in the mid-nineteenth century that appropriate ornament, although not always useful, was important—people found it appealing, even necessary, contrary to the dictates of "great authorities" that they should not.[7] In Wharton's view, fresco paintings, such as those in the interiors at Pompeii, along with paneling and tapestries, were the best ways to decorate walls. There was the logic of their evolution, not only as decoration but also, in the case of tapestries, or wood or stone wall panels, as insulation against cold in the North or heat in the warmer climates. She felt these ideas could easily be adapted to the then "modern rooms." She disapproved of the large expanses of glass being used in windows at the time, and thought that the division of glass panes with mullions was necessary to make the traditional distinction between the exterior and interior, and that these also acted as part of the wall design: "A large unbroken sheet of plate-glass interrupts the decorative scheme of the room, just as in verse, if the distances between the rhymes are so great that the ear cannot connect them, the continuity of sound is interrupted."[8]

At the turn of the twentieth century, artists were striving to connect their art with the minds of their viewers in a series of movements that were to impact not only fine art, but also furniture, interiors, and architecture. Color extended beyond decoration to define space or function. Working in Paris, Marc Chagall developed a style that bordered on the surreal, disassociating color from object to give it symbolic meaning. Picasso's persistent use of blue up to 1904 evokes sadness or despair. A few years later he, along with other artists such as Braque, turned to cubism. Moving from a fixed perspective, realistic forms were fragmented, rearranged in simple or complex inter-

1. Edith Wharton, *The Decoration of Houses*, 14.
2. Ibid, 14.
3. Ibid, 68.
4. Ibid, 30.
5. Ibid, 32.
6. Wharton, however, disagreed with Ruskin in her preference for classical symmetry over the picturesque asymmetry of Gothic architecture.
7. John Ruskin, *The Stones of Venice*, 38.
8. *The Decoration of Houses*, 70.

locking planes, and reassembled to express a new dimensional reality of what the mind, rather than the eye, sees.

The De Stijl movement, which was founded in 1917 and was to last only about fourteen years, sought to create a new order out of the turmoil of the First World War by removing the old focus on the individual, breaking with history and tradition, and creating a vocabulary of form based on the geometry of planes and linear elements that could be universally understood. Among the founders was Dutch architect and painter Theo van Doesburg, who was influenced by theosophy, a contemporary movement based on a philosophy evolving from Oriental religions and a spiritual view of the nature of the universe. The color palette was reduced to basic primary colors: yellow, representing vertical rays; blue, the opposite, the "horizontal firmament," as in the heavens; and red, the union of yellow and blue in the cosmic sense of antiquity rather than pigment mixtures.[9] Dutch artist Piet Mondrian adhered to this philosophy of red, yellow, and blue, with black, white, and gray separating or defining the colors. Reputed as having an aversion to green, Mondrian supposedly went so far as to choose to sit in a chair that excluded views of nature.

The ideas of the artists Mondrian and van Doesburg carried over to furniture and architecture. A member of the De Stijl group, Dutch architect and cabinetmaker Gerrit Rietveld combined simple geometric forms and primary colors in his red and blue chair of 1917. Rietveld's Schroeder House of 1924 bridged the concept of chair to structure, where smooth, planar surfaces and walls of gray or white were offset by accents of red and yellow, and movable wall panels separated the rooms.

Scientists and psychologists were also entering the picture. Building on the works of Goethe and Chevreul, numerous published reports on studies of color perception, phenomena, and therapy were being conducted in the early twentieth century that paralleled the new exploration of color by artists. In his Color Course and Seminar at the Bauhaus, Kandinsky explored, in addition to color and form, the psychological, physiological, and philosophical aspects of color, leading to its disassociation from objects and perception in an abstract way. His book *On the Spiritual in Art* (1912) expresses his views on the evils of materialism in society and commercialism in art and the necessity to refocus the artist to a spiritual awakening—to rely on internal expression to communicate feelings rather than solely on "beauty of color and form."[10] He admired the boldness of artists of the time, such as Matisse, Cézanne, and Picasso, for their individual senses of color.[11]

The psychological aspects of color, as well as its ability to advance or recede, create a powerful effect in art. In addition to the affinity of color to certain forms as gathered

9. Based on the writings of mathematician M.H.J. Schoen-maekers in "The New Image of the World," 1915. Kenneth Frampton, *Modern Architecture*, 142; John Gage, *Color and Culture*, 257.

10. *Kandinsky, Complete Writings on Art.* "On the Spiritual in Art," 197.
11. Ibid, 151, 152. Kandinsky notes Cezanne's free expression in contrasting warm and cool colors, along with chromatic value changes that gave life to inanimate objects; Matisse's exaggeration of color; and the freedom of Picasso, who, if color interfered with form in his cubist paintings, "throws it overboard and paints a picture in browns and whites."

I and the Village, Marc Chagall. In this dreamlike scene the artist depicts himself with a green face, which is thought to represent a longing for the fields of his native Russia. (*Colour,* 210; *Smithsonian Magazine* (n.d.), article by Robert Wernick: "In his tenth decade Marc Chagall's brush still danced.")

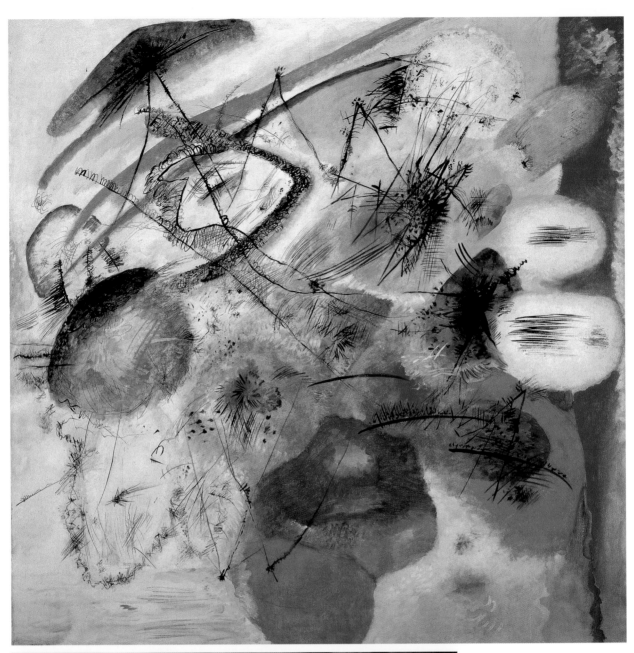

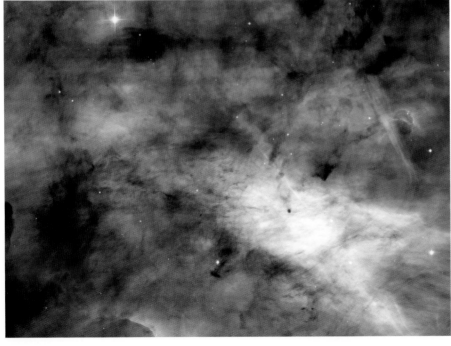

in his Bauhaus survey—red to the square, blue to the circle, yellow to the triangle—Kandinsky placed emphasis on color in terms of warm/cool and light/dark and shared Goethe's fascination with yellow and blue.[12] To his eyes, a dark color such as blue, when contained in a circle, spiraled inward, while yellow revolved outward, perhaps like rays of the sun. Combining yellow and blue diluted the movement of both and resulted in the calmness of green.

History has established a connection between the arts and sciences. Scientists Newton, Chevreul, and Ostwald opened new directions in color theory, and, in his *Point and Line to Plane* (Munich 1926), Kandinsky connected geometry not only to art and form, but also to music, nature, and science.

We often refer to an "eye for color" or "ear for music." The combination of the two senses dates to ancient Greece in the realization that color and music could be organized along mathematical scales. Likewise, the vocabularies of art and music are often interchangeable.[13] They include such expressions as "orchestral color" or "coloratura"—a soprano with as wide and agile a vocal range as a color chart with all its tonal and chromatic variations. Kandinsky compared rhythm in music to points and lines forming compositions in art and architecture. In his writings, he associated color with various instruments: "light blue . . . the flute, dark blue, the cello . . . darker still . . . , the double bass"; the darkest blue, "the deep notes of the organ"; "absolute green . . . the quiet, expansive middle register of the violin"; bright red, "the sound of a fanfare, in which the tuba can also be heard"; red turning to orange, "a viola playing a largo"; and violet, the mournful sound of a bassoon.[14]

The French architect, Le Corbusier—born Charles-Edouard Jeanneret in Switzerland in 1887—was known for his furniture designs in addition to architecture. He had other facets to his career as well, as a writer, artist, wallpaper designer, and interior decorator. He viewed interiors with the same eye for color and composition as his paintings and oversaw all the details, from carpet and draperies to furniture and lighting. He designed a range of wallpapers in forty-three colors for a Swiss firm and also developed paint colors.

Le Corbusier loved drawing as a child. During his career as an architect he continued to paint daily, and his work in both areas shows cubist influence. As a young man, he took the grand tour of Europe in the spirit of Inigo Jones and copied great works of art, such as Giotto's frescoes. Letters to his art teacher express an acute awareness of color, as in his apology for an exuberant watercolor painted after a storm: "Please don't come down too hard on this small impression of the Pallio [*sic*] Square in Siena. You know that Siena is the city of colors. It takes little—a storm comes, it lights up all the

Previous spread: The Schroeder House.
Opposite, above: *Black Lines No. 189,* 1913, Wassily Kandinsky.
Opposite, below: The Swan Nebula, NASA photo taken from the Hubble Space Telescope. A comparison of Kandinsky's 1913 painting with a photograph of outer space taken in 2002 exhibits common forces of energy and color.

12. Ibid, 163,179. Kandinsky writes, "In the most general terms, the warmth or coldness of a color is due to its inclination toward yellow or toward blue." In addition to spiraling outward and inward, warm yellow moves forward, while cool blue recedes. Kandinsky also points out that the "incompatibility" of various geometric forms with colors could be interesting, a new kind of harmony, perhaps similar to that found in discordant music.
13. *Color and Culture*, 235. The nineteenth-century artist's palette was often compared to the keyboard. In the resulting artistic creation, as in music, emotion is evoked.

hues like a fresh watercolor, it leaves behind some big black clouds strewn on a raw green evening sky, while the quenched earth exhales its bliss in marvelous pink vapors . . . one may have let oneself be carried away and give in to such resonant harmonies."[15] In a letter from Pisa, he verbally painted another vivid description of the perception of color on surfaces, which included an awareness of the "painter's hour," when colors metamorphose at dusk:

> At six o'clock in the evening, the Duomo is a magic play of colors, a distillation of yellows in all hues and intensities, of ivory white and black patina, all that against an ultramarine so intense that, if you stare at it long enough, you see black. The part where the baptistery casts its shadow is all gentle vibration of rich yellows, of red inlaid marbles lighting up, of blue marble turning darker: it is the triumph of flat surfaces, vibrant and in gentle conversation—7 in the evening, this Duomo is even more beautiful than ever; what tones! It's some sort of brown, some sort of blue, such quiet! Behind me the sky is orange and mauve, the green in the doors is dead, yellow marbles come out, they are natural sienna, while the columns are a white pink, like the petal of a wild rose. Under the small arches of the vaults, you would think that you see the frescoes next door (in the camposanto), the beautiful frescoes in gold and red; the diffuse shadow projected by the colonnettes is emerald green, and the black marble is gray like the neck of some birds. In this andante burst out the three mosaics, their gold shimmering with the most beautiful sunset, while the virgin's green dress vibrates gently. The crimsons have disappeared.[16]

Le Corbusier studied interiors at Fontainebleau and Versailles. He admired French Empire and Directoire furniture as well as more provincial styles. He viewed desks and case pieces for storage as architecture, and he united furniture and architecture by developing cabinets in standard modules that could be painted either the wall color to become part of the wall or in contrasting colors to stand out as furniture. He loved white—perhaps stemming from a fondness for the whitewashed buildings on Greek islands—and he believed in using it for interiors, but noted that it should also be balanced with "a well regulated polychromy."[17]

Color became an integral part of one of his most famous homes, the Villa Savoye, a pristine, white structure that was raised on thin columns, or *pilotis*, with an exterior wall at the base painted green as a visual connection with the lawn and trees beyond. Color was used architecturally in the interior as well, with white walls interrupted by planes of pink, blue, and red ocher. In an unexpected playfulness of color, he brought a

14. *Kandinsky, Complete Writings on Art*, 91, 182, 183, 187-189; John Gage, *Color and Culture*, 236. Kandinsky, who played the cello, admired the atonal music of composer Arnold Schoenberg and noted its parallel to abstract art.

15. Stanislaus von Moos, *Le Corbusier Before Le Corbusier*, 31. Letter to Charles L'Eplattenier, quoted in Sekler, "Early Drawings," 1977.

16. Ibid, 32. Quoted from Gresleri, "Viaggia in Toscano," 1987.

17. James Ackerman, *The Villa*, 272. Quoted from "Oeuvre Complete," 1937.

hint of sky into an interior corridor by painting one wall a vivid blue, which cast a lighter blue reflection on the opposite white wall. Gazing at a red ocher wall in the boy's bedroom results in an after-image of green on the white wall in an adjacent bathroom. In his earlier travels, Le Corbusier was struck by the complementary colors of a red garment in front of a green door, and perhaps it played a role in his use of pink and red ocher on interior wall planes to complement the green foliage surrounding the villa. The windows in Pompeii that framed views of atrium gardens may have inspired him to cut windows in the walls around the second-floor terrace and roof garden of the villa to frame views of nature as if they were paintings.

Another connection between color and architecture is the way colors advance and recede in space. In general, warm colors (red, yellow, orange) tend to advance, while cool colors (blues and greens) seem to recede, but other factors may alter this rule. Very bright, cool colors can advance more than darker or less saturated warm ones. In *The Art of Color*, Johannes Itten mentioned other points to consider, such as the contrast effect of a background color or, in the case of more than one color, the quantity or proportion that may cause either one to advance or recede. Excellent examples of how geometric objects in color advance, recede, or rotate in space can be seen in the work of early-twentieth-century Russian avant-garde artists. Kasimir Malevich's *Suprematist Painting* (1915) illustrates Itten's principles in showing a blue rectangle placed over a background of black and white; the blue moves forward on white and recedes on black. In the same painting, thin black lines on a white background appear to recede compared to larger black geometric shapes, which advance as their size increases.

Artists have manipulated color and space in other ways. In traditional paintings, neutral or cool background colors in portraits added an illusion of depth, or called attention to the subject's expression or luxurious details of clothing or jewels. In the twentieth-century artist Mark Rothko's painting *Number One* (1953), one can almost feel the heat of the red as it advances toward the viewer. In Jacques-Louis David's portrait of Mme. Trudaine (c. 1792), the viewer can also feel the red background push forward, but here the color also conveys an inner turmoil of the subject, despite her placid expression. David's portrait of Mme. de Verninac (1799), with its cool neutral background reinforces the calm demeanor of subject. A twentieth-century interpretation of the serenity of green can be seen in Barnett Newman's *Concord* (1949).

Many of the principles used by artists to manipulate color and form in a painting can be useful in achieving a broader perspective in the approach to color for interior spaces.

Page 157, above: Villa Savoye. A blue wall in the corridor casts its reflection on the opposite white wall. In the bedroom an after-image of green will appear if focus is shifted from the red ocher wall to the white wall of the bathroom behind the door.

Page 157, below: A picturesque view is captured through a framed opening on the wall of the Villa Savoye's roof terrace.

Opposite: *Suprematist Painting*, 1915, Kasimir Malevich.

Opposite: *Portrait of Mme. Trudaine,* c.1792, Jacques-Louis David.
Above: *Number One,* 1953, Mark Rothko.
Following spread, left: *Portrait of Mme. de Verninac,* 1799, Jacques-Louis David.
Following spread, right: *Concord,* 1949, Barnett Newman.

Barnett Newman 1949

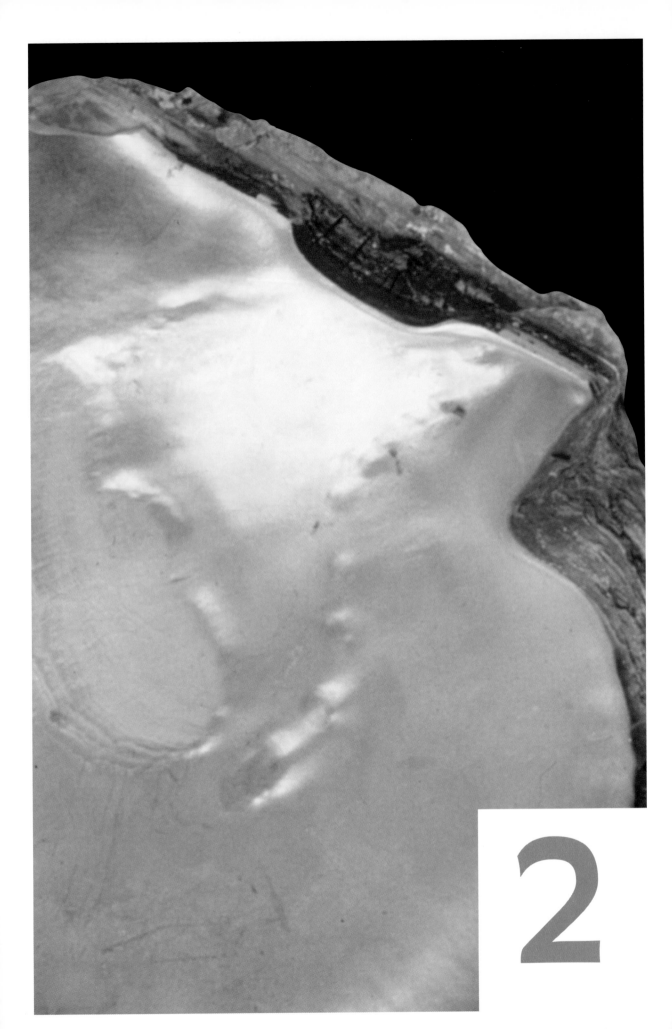

2

OBSERVATIONS ON THE INTERACTION OF COLOR by scientists and artists that date back to the nineteenth century, or even to antiquity, can provide designers with knowledge that may be put to practical use today: demonstrations by Chevreul and Albers on the capricious behavior of colors; Itten's concept of freedom achieved through the use of objective criteria; and the gray scales of Ostwald and Munsell as a reminder of the importance of neutral values.

Color can be luminous or anemic, expand or contract, advance or recede, appear lightweight or heavy, warm or cool. Too many colors will confuse; too few may disturb. In addition to physical variables that affect the perception of color, people's attitudes toward color vary greatly. Some prefer bright, vivid colors; others pastels; still others prefer a neutral palette. Light colors may be favored over dark, warm colors over cool, high over low contrast, subtle textures over bold patterns and prints.

Given the extensive variety of possibilities, color selection and its distribution around a room should be a studied rather than haphazard process. Keeping the value of good instincts in mind, a designer must proceed with logical decisions—based on knowledge and on training under qualified professionals—in order to avoid unpleasant surprises and costly errors. The designer provides a color scheme that a client can live with and enjoy but, at the same time, must satisfy his or her own sense of values. This may require educating the client. There are no easy formulas, but knowledge of general rules and guidelines provides a basis for these decisions. Rules often can be broken with splendid results, but this requires a level of skill to do well.

Tonal Distribution

A fundamental principle that goes back to the earliest interiors is the concept of nature's distribution of tonal values; people feel more comfortable in a room with a light ceiling, medium walls, and dark floors, which parallel the tonal values of the sky, foliage, and earth. However, there are numerous variations on and exceptions to the theory: the walls of the black bedroom at Boscotrecase, dark wood paneling in traditional rooms that date back to the sixteenth century and are still popular, and contemporary spaces that have dark walls and lighter floors.

Chromatic Distribution

A second general rule follows nature's distribution of vivid color in its accessories, such as birds and flowers, and is also allied to Munsell's theory that strong colors should not overpower weaker ones. The guideline states that the largest areas of a room, such as floor, walls, and ceiling, should be the most neutral. As size is decreased, chromatic

Color Schemes: Theory to Practice

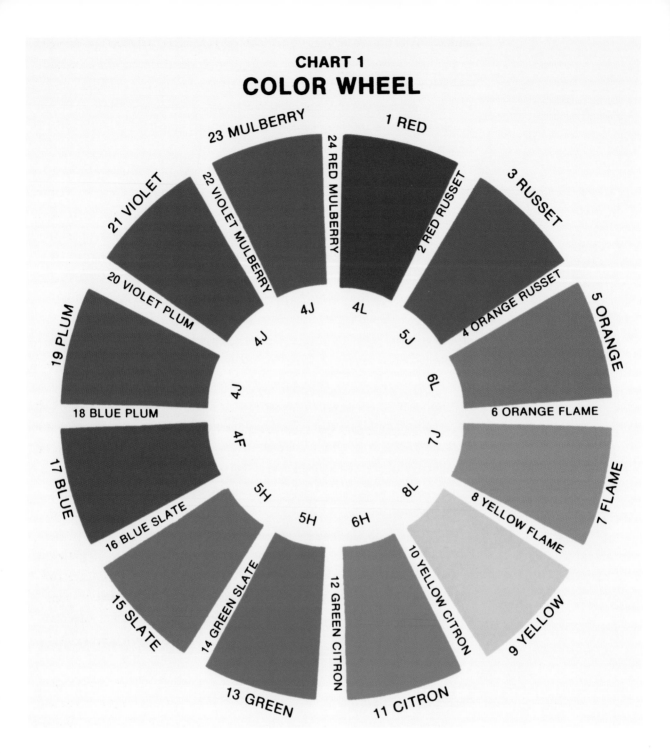

CHART 1
COLOR WHEEL

1 RED
23 MULBERRY
24 RED MULBERRY
3 RUSSET
22 VIOLET MULBERRY
2 RED RUSSET
21 VIOLET
4 ORANGE RUSSET
20 VIOLET PLUM
5 ORANGE
19 PLUM
6 ORANGE FLAME
18 BLUE PLUM
7 FLAME
17 BLUE
8 YELLOW FLAME
16 BLUE SLATE
10 YELLOW CITRON
15 SLATE
9 YELLOW
14 GREEN SLATE
12 GREEN CITRON
13 GREEN
11 CITRON

4J   4L
4J   5J
4J   6L
4F   7J
5H   8L
5H   6H

Page 164: The iridescence of mother of pearl.

Above: The 12-color wheel of pigments developed by the New York
School of Interior Design in the 1940s shows primary, secondary, and
tertiary colors in full chromatic values. The names between the colors
are the quaternaries, made by mixing a primary or secondary color with
its adjacent tertiary.

value can be increased. Furniture or draperies can be brighter, and small upholstered items or accessories and other accents can be the most chromatic. Many successful interiors break this rule, but one should be aware that there is a chromatic range on walls in which, depending on the light, an intense color can become intolerable.

Color Harmonies

There are various approaches based on the color wheel that can be used as guides to create a harmonious color scheme for a room:

Neutral or Monotone. This is a color scheme in which a single neutral in the same tonal and chromatic value is used for major areas. For many years, this was used most often as a background in galleries and retail stores. Today, many residential interiors are almost entirely neutral, with a range of values—schemes of white and black, beige, taupe, or gray. Psychological effects are important: an all-beige room may feel too warm; gray, too morose; all-white, chilling in winter. Neutrals can be surprisingly difficult to work with; when they are placed together, subtle color differences will stand out. The effect of a neutral or monotonal scheme can be antiseptic, or it can be elegantly simple and serene if enough texture, value accents, and/or subtle color are added.

Monochromatic. In this scheme, major areas of a room are treated with various tonal and chromatic values of a single color. This provides a restful scheme and is often recommended for small rooms. The objective is to have enough contrast in major areas: among wall, drapery, floor, and ceiling values as well as between the walls and furniture. Tonal variety can range from almost white, to medium values, to dark, including almost-brown in warm colors, and dark grays to black in cool colors. Texture is essential in order to prevent monotony, and subtle pattern can add interest.

Neutral and One Color. This scheme can be energizing as well as more effective than using a lot of color. Using a range of tonal variations of the color and contrast in neutral values can add visual variety. The neutral and one-color scheme is often seen in stage design, where the eye is immediately drawn to a single color on a neutral background. An example in a room is the abstracted rose on the white closets in the Mackintosh bedroom.

Analogous. This scheme involves three colors that are adjacent on a twelve-color wheel, with varying tonal and chromatic values—for example, blue-green, green, and yellow-green.[1] Values can range from off-white to very dark, and from almost-neutral to bright. In reality, in order to avoid monotony, most analogous schemes would have a touch of the complementary color, in this case, red. An expanded analogous scheme— that is, five adjacent colors on a twelve-color wheel—can be a little more energetic. For

1. On the previous chart the named colors would be slate, green, and citron.

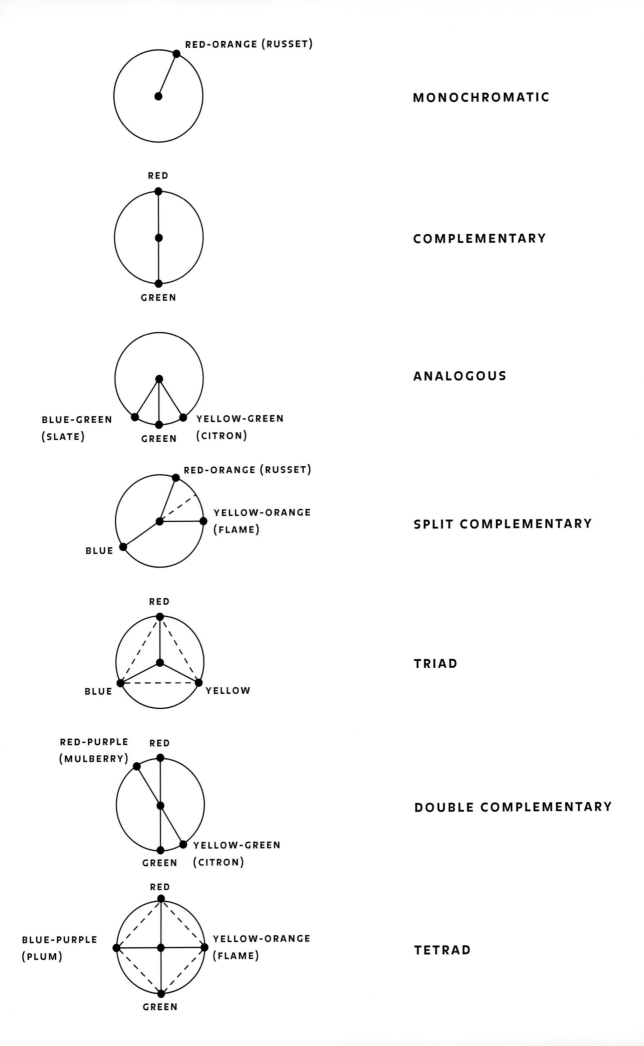

RED-ORANGE (RUSSET)

MONOCHROMATIC

RED

GREEN

COMPLEMENTARY

ANALOGOUS

BLUE-GREEN
(SLATE)
GREEN
YELLOW-GREEN
(CITRON)

RED-ORANGE (RUSSET)

YELLOW-ORANGE
(FLAME)

BLUE

SPLIT COMPLEMENTARY

RED

TRIAD

BLUE
YELLOW

RED-PURPLE
(MULBERRY)
RED

DOUBLE COMPLEMENTARY

YELLOW-GREEN
GREEN
(CITRON)

RED

BLUE-PURPLE
(PLUM)
YELLOW-ORANGE
(FLAME)

TETRAD

GREEN

example, a three-color scheme of blue, blue-green, and green could be expanded to include yellow-green and yellow. When using this many colors, it is important that no more than two or three should predominate in large areas, with the remaining ones used as accents. However, overdoing a single color in major areas of a room—green walls, upholstery, and drapery with other colors merely as accents—can be tiresome.

Complementary. A scheme comprised of two colors opposite each other on the color wheel, this is thought to provide an ideal balance in a room, because it always includes a warm and a cool color. These colors in turn include all three primaries of pigment: in a red/green scheme, green contains yellow and blue; and in a blue/orange scheme, orange contains red and yellow. It conforms to theorists' observations that the eye searches for the complement of a color and, if not satisfied, will create it with an after-image to restore equilibrium.

In theory, complementary colors are usually more harmonious if they incline toward each other on the color wheel. Thus, in a red/green scheme, red that fringes on red-orange would work better with green that leans toward yellow; conversely, red that leans toward blue would better complement a green that leans toward blue-green. Proportions in a complementary scheme should not be equal. It is better when one color, in various tonal and chromatic variations, predominates; for example, instead of a "red/green" room, it is better to have variations of red with added greens, and of course, a range of neutrals.

Split Complementary. This scheme includes a color and the two colors adjacent to its complement on a twelve-color wheel. Instead of red and green, a split complementary scheme would include red with yellow-green and blue-green. Its appeal in this case may lie in the combination of red with two tertiary colors, which in theory have more subtlety and sophistication than a primary (red) and secondary (green).

Double Complementary. On a twelve-color wheel, this would contain two sets of colors opposite each other—for example, red and red-orange with green and blue-green. This combines the visual stimulus of complements with the restraint of analogous colors, a contradiction that, if skillfully applied, can provide more appeal than either scheme.

Triad. This scheme is comprised of three equidistant colors on a twelve-color wheel. As in all schemes, it would include a range of tonal and chromatic values in varying proportions, with one or two colors dominant. A triad of primaries—red, yellow, and blue—makes a strong statement but could be jarring in large amounts in a room, with each color competing for attention. A more sophisticated approach would be a triad of tertiaries—for example, red-orange, yellow-green, and blue-purple.[2]

Opposite: Color harmony: various approaches to schemes based on the color wheel. (Monochromatic, complementary, analogous, split complementary, double complementary, triad, tetrad.)

2. Russet, citron, and plum.

MUNSELL® STUDENT CHART

HUE

Munsell 10.0 YR — NYSID Color Flame

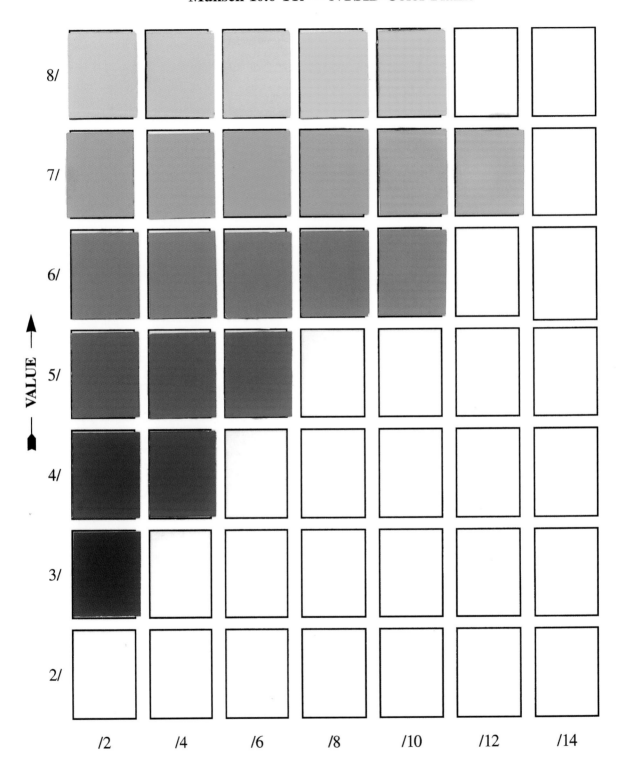

VALUE →

8/
7/
6/
5/
4/
3/
2/

/2   /4   /6   /8   /10   /12   /14

Opposite: Tonal and chromatic values of a tertiary color, yellow-orange (flame) in a chart based on the Munsell system modified for the New York School of Interior Design.

Above: Comparison with the yellow-orange color chart shows a range of tonal and chromatic values, from lighter tints on the walls and drapery, to stronger chroma at medium value on the sofa, to dark browns and black. Light neutrals are added in whites of the side chair, lamp shade, pillows and painting. The scheme is primarily monochromatic, or one color, with accents of analogous blue and green. Although the walls are plain, the room is rich in texture and pattern, which is carried vertically from the sofa and foliage on the pillows to the painting. Dark values are also connected vertically, from the black coffee tables to the center pillow to the peacock. The green leaf accessories on the coffee tables make another visual connection to greens in the painting. (Sarah Morris of Colefax & Fowler, and Cathy Kincaid)

Tetrad. This scheme is comprised of four equidistant colors on a twelve-color wheel. It always includes a primary color; a secondary color, which is its complement; and two tertiary colors, which are complementary. A tetrad scheme with a primary of red would have a secondary of green and tertiaries of yellow-orange and blue-purple.[3]

The more complex schemes, if properly used, can have a degree of subtlety, the effect of "nature's colouring" admired by Dresser, or the sophisticated layering of colors in the court dress of ancient Japan. If improperly done, they can have the unpleasant effect of Wharton's too many "voices talking at the same time," or the colors may simply cancel each other out.

Coordinating a Color Scheme

Colors selected for an interior are meant to provide a visually harmonious space for the inhabitants. This harmony can be described as a pleasing arrangement of parts, which can be either languorous or exhilarating, soothing or discordant. The perception of harmony, in vision as well as in music, varies as greatly from person to person as it has from age to age; there are no absolute rules for either artist or designer. It is often said that in reality there are no good or bad colors, but how they are used makes them appealing or unattractive. Tonal and chromatic value, texture, and their proportion and distribution around a room are ingredients that can make a space succeed or fail.

Architectural Features

Walls are the largest area a designer has to deal with, but they are too often an after-thought, or far down on the list in the decision-making process. One should resist the inclination to think primarily in terms of fabric and furniture when planning a color scheme and instead consider first the architecture, orientation, and light as well as existing materials that are to remain in the room.

Building styles vary widely, and color can be evaluated in terms of traditional or contemporary settings, or a mixture of both. Recalling Wharton's dictum, what is the architecture of the room in terms of wall planes, voids, and solids? Is it traditional with floor, wall, and ceiling planes separated by graceful molding and framed door openings? Or is it a contemporary space where rooms flow into one another without definitive divisions? Are windows small, admitting little light or view, or are they large expanses of glass where, in reality, the view furnishes the room? Other consider-ations in deciding on wall colors are: the orientation of the room, keeping in mind that warm colors are often used for rooms facing north, and cool colors for those facing south or west; the purpose of the room—for living, dining, sleeping, bathing;

---

3. Red, green, flame, and plum.

Previous spread, left: Walls glazed in a combination of bronze with blue and green are carried into the seating and provide a restful analogous scheme. The essential touch of white is present, while a little purple in the floral arrangement complements the golden tones in the wall and picture frame. (Debra Blair)

Previous spread, right: This fresh interpretation successfully ignores the general rule that complementary colors should incline towards each other on the color wheel. Here pale, yellow-green draperies contrast with darker, bluish red chairs. The blue in this picture next to the draperies, and the russet in the carpet, add an analogous touch on a vertical and horizontal level. (Robert Couturier)

Above: Nature's bloom of color is reflected in warm reds and yellows complemented by cool greens. The carpet is appropriately grounded by a strong red color, while the light background of the chintz covering the chairs is suitable to their graceful forms. Dark values in the artwork are carried down to the coffee and end tables. (Parish-Hadley)

Above: Molding can be painted out to achieve a subtle textural effect as a background for contemporary furniture, or it can be highlighted to call attention to its detail in a traditional setting. As Edith Wharton noted, rooms that are architecturally balanced and perfectly detailed can stand on their own with little or no furnishings. Warm yellow walls and wood tones are cooled down with exquisite white plasterwork and cool blues and greens in paint-ings of outdoor scenes. The dark void of the fireplace opening is balanced vertically by dark values in the painting above. (Kirlington Park Room, The Metropolitan Museum of Art)

Above: Neutral rooms can be restful but also gain subtle energy with value and texture. Here light, medium, and dark values are well balanced around the room. Textures and patterns are quietly visible in the abstract floral carpet, checkered drapery, muted stripe on the sofa and club chairs, and beaded pillows. Light creates texture on the wall plane by adding shadows to the moldings. The sculptured console table and turned arms and legs of the desk chair contrast with the simple lines of the desk. (Mariette Himes Gomez)

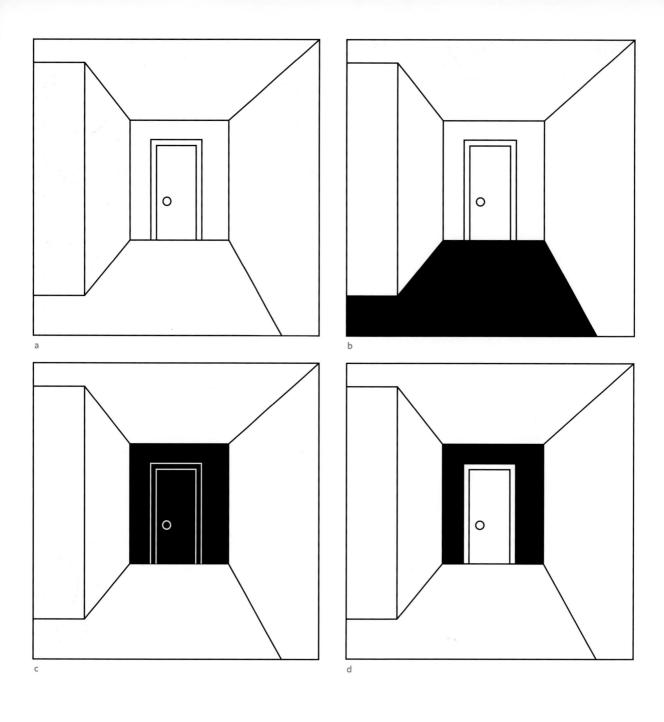

a

b

c

d

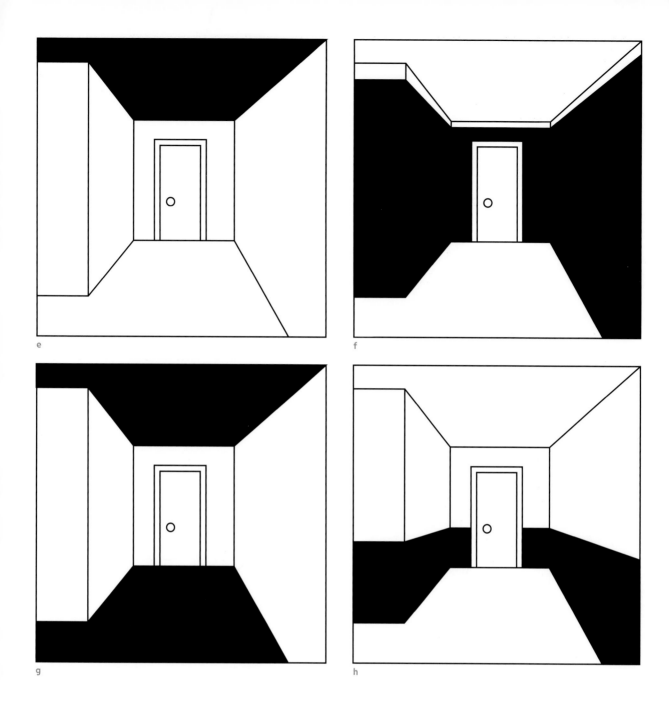

Sketches of rooms with architectural problems that are helped or hindered by application of color: a–b) effects of a light or dark floor; c) how a dark wall shortens a long corridor; d) how high contrast focuses attention on the door; e) how a dark ceiling lowers it; f) how a ceiling can be made to appear higher by carrying the light color down into the crown; g) how a sandwich effect is created by dark floor and ceiling; h) how a room is cut in half by highly contrasting colors on the upper wall and dado;

Following page: i) how a room is cut in half by all dark values at table level; j) how dark values can be carried vertically with art work.

i

j

the frequency of use—heavily used or merely a passageway; and the room's relationship to adjacent ones.

Traditional rooms have distinct boundaries between the floor and wall; the door or window and wall; and the wall and ceiling. Moldings used in these interiors create ideal boundaries to stop and start different colors in transition from floor to ceiling or from room to room. A common practice in eighteenth-century English and French interiors with good architectural proportions was to contrast moldings or other details with the wall or highlight them with gilding. In rooms with poor architectural features, doors or window frames that are off center are best painted to match the wall in order to camouflage their irregularity. Likewise, windows that are off center are better furnished with draperies that blend in rather than contrast with the wall. Balance may also be achieved with furniture placement.

High ceilings in traditional rooms are often painted a dark color to minimize their height. In a room with a dado, the height can be made to appear lower by using contrasting colors on the upper and lower portions of the wall. In a room with a low ceiling, painting it a dark color will weigh down on the room, and contrasting horizontal divisions will appear to cut the room in half. In a similar way, a light wall between a dark ceiling and floor can result in an uncomfortable sandwich effect.

The finishing connections of moldings are, for the most part, nonexistent in contemporary interiors, which may be one of the reasons for the popularity of neutral and monochromatic schemes for these spaces. Walls in contemporary rooms that are painted with contrasting colors are unsuccessful when they are based on arbitrary decisions rather than a full understanding of the architecture. Where moldings are absent, a contrast or change of color on walls, or between the walls and ceiling, will call attention to imperfect or uneven connections where the wall and ceiling planes meet. Other problems arise with doors and small windows that are poorly balanced, and unsightly heating units. In terms of furnishings, it can also be jarring to see the juxta-position of antique furniture on three sides of a room and a contemporary cityscape through a large, uncovered window on the fourth.

Color and Light

In selecting colors for rooms, it is essential to work from large samples, holding them vertically if they will be seen on walls, and to view them under different lighting conditions. When using a highly reflective color such as yellow on a wall, the color theorist Faber Birren's advice is to "dilute the paint with as much as fifty per cent white . . ." to have the finished wall color look the same as the small sample.[4] When

4. Faber Birren, *Color for Interiors*, 20.

looking at a small sample of bright color, one should always keep in mind that its intensity will accelerate as its size is increased. Tertiary colors, which are more subtle and sophisticated than primaries and secondaries, can be a better choice for large wall areas, provided they are not too dark or chromatic.

Light can never be ignored. Dark or vivid colors work well in darker rooms. In traditional interiors, bright colors were used on walls and in textiles, but the rooms had small windows, often set into thick walls, and were lighted at night by candles. In historic restorations, in which rooms are shown under contemporary lighting conditions, the historically accurate colors that appear garish to our eyes would have been more pleasing in their time.

In rooms with large windows, color on walls may throw the proportions of the room off balance. This balance will also be reversed as the window wall changes from light during the day to dark at night. Although windows have the distinct advantage of admitting light and a view, bright or dark colors can look harsh in strong light, pastels too delicate, and very light colors completely washed out. In this case, color may be more appropriate on a freestanding wall or furniture and in artwork and accessories.

Adjacent Rooms

In a progression through adjacent rooms, contrast and change are good, but the transition must be coherent. Wall changes, as from a dark entry hall to a light living room, can be pleasant as long as there is a logical place to start and stop the colors and there is some relief with neutrals. Caution should be used in making abrupt changes in the flooring of connecting rooms, especially in small spaces. For example, if there is a change of material from wood to wall-to-wall carpet, it is often best to keep the color constant or have only a slight value change.

Texture

A designer works with man-made as well as natural materials, both having widely different characteristics. Color is a major consideration, but an awareness of texture and value is equally important. Everything in nature has some form of texture, and rooms without texture can appear lifeless. People have different preferences: some are drawn to an old, weathered look; others, to shiny, pristine, smooth surfaces. Organic materials such as wood and marble have a character of their own, and their beauty is in their distinct color variation and eccentric patterns. Graining in wood can be subtle or bold. When plastic laminates were first introduced, the colors were solid or photo-

Opposite: A watercolor rendering by the late Mark Hampton of an enfilade, a passage through adjacent rooms, shows the contrast of warm wood colors with cool blues.

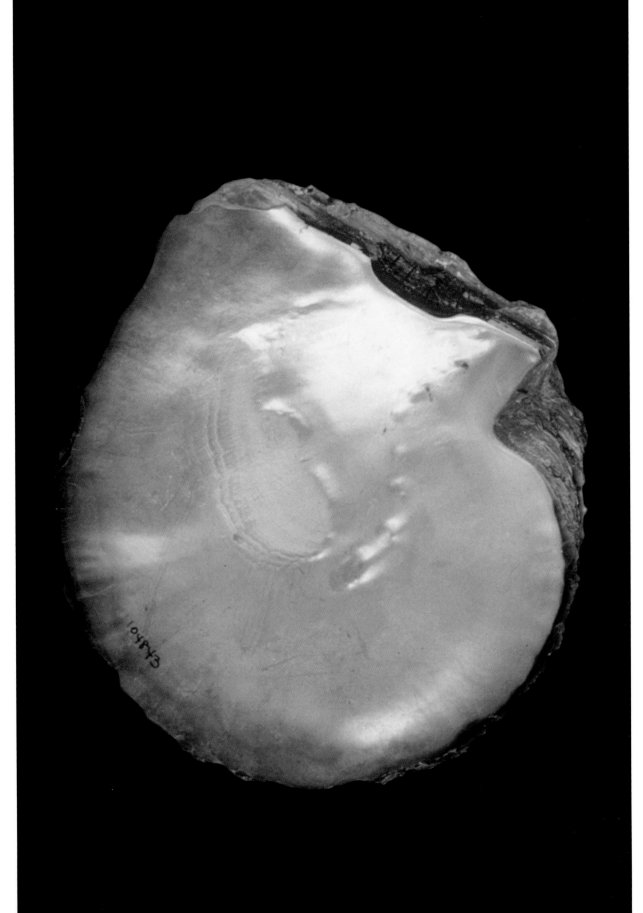

graphic copies of wood and marble; the obvious imitations were unappealing and were replaced by more successful abstract interpretations of natural textures.

Viewing distance to the textured surface is very important. Small patterns and other elements that appear highly textured on a close-up viewing of a sample can look solid as one moves away. Coarsely woven or textured fabrics look darker than the original yarn used in weaving because of shadows caused by the uneven surface. Even the smooth white walls of a room will have places that are lighter or darker due to shadows caused by a light source, or they can be tinted by light reflected from nearby colored objects.

Contrast of Textures

As we have learned from the theorists, a dark object next to a lighter one will heighten their contrast. A small object next to a large one will do the same. This principle holds true for rough and smooth textures and for scale and proportion in patterns. Although some variation is necessary between textures, care should generally be taken with sharp contrasts. A smooth fabric or surface next to highly textured one will exaggerate their difference, as will a solid color next to a print. A print or floral fabric may look better either with some textured fabric nearby or with a combination of a small geometric pattern or stripe together with textures on other surfaces.

Texture on Walls

Faux finishes—the painter's way of imitating natural materials such as wood, marble or tortoiseshell—have been used for centuries and are still popular. Walls or other surfaces can be given an added textural dimension by distressing, antiquing, or glazing. A darker glaze over a lighter wall color will give more depth and make a surface breathe.[5] The use of slightly different tints or values of a color can also create texture or a subtle iridescent effect.

In the eighteenth century the French heightened moldings with touches of color to give them the appearance of texture. Robert Adam painted shallow moldings white to give the illusion of added height against pastel walls or ceilings. Painting a room with low-profile paneling and moldings all white can diminish the effect of shade and shadow, which was the original intent of molding. Whichever technique is used, subtlety works best in producing the desired effect.

Iridescence

People have always been drawn to shine and sparkle, to the sun, gold, silver, gems,

Opposite: Lustrous or iridescent materials that reflect light have had universal appeal since antiquity—gold, silver, gems, pearls, or velvets and silks in brilliant colors—and their popularity continues to this day. Although mother of pearl is colorless, it contains minute grooves that diffract, or bend, the light striking its uneven surface which is then scattered and results in a reflection of soft tints.

5. This is the same concept that artists use in landscapes where dark colors in the foreground that fade into light colors in the background give the painting depth.

metals, the play of light and shadow, and the iridescence of silks and velvets. The luster of silks, damasks, or iridescent fabrics is diminished against plain walls, and the same holds true for fine art and antiques. Old master paintings are more favorably seen against a background of traditional moldings or panels, richly colored damasks, or walls with some color instead of plain ones, a practice followed by many museums.

Smooth surfaces are often perceived as lacking texture, but texture can be visual as well as tactile. For example, silk, glass, or metal can have a texture created by reflections cast on their surfaces.

Mirrors made of antique glass whose surfaces are mottled through corrosion cast soft reflections. Although large, modern mirrors have the benefit of expanding a space, they can also cast harsh reflections, and care should be taken with their placement. In an interior, every object is seen against another object or surface, not only in color and value, but also in texture.

Contrast

All contrast effects are relative. A line appears long or short according to its relation to a shorter or longer line. A gray tone appears light or dark depending on whether it is compared with something darker or lighter. In a pictorial composition, a large, dark form becomes more significant if a small, bright form counteracts it. Many of these principles of contrast can be applied on a larger scale to interiors.

Tonal Values

While changes in tonal values can highlight good architectural details in a room, subtle or high contrasts can achieve serenity or drama. Strong contrast calls attention to form and shape. In an interior, a jump from a tonal value of one to a tonal value of ten, unless done with a trained eye, can be jarring. A more gentle transition incorporates the buffer of an intermediate range of values to cushion the impact and hold the composition together. Vital to the composition of a well-designed, perfectly balanced room is the awareness, as in art, of positive and negative space created by these values.

Before planning a color scheme it is important to consider existing materials and to note the transition of architectural materials—floor to base to wall to crown molding (if it exists) to ceiling. The integration of background (architecture and walls) and foreground (furniture and accessories) in a relationship of positive and negative space should be planned with both color and value in mind. Ceiling height is important as well. Verticality is preferred—that is, the height should be sufficient in relation to

A touch of color and a range of medium to dark values in furnishings and accessories add depth and definition to this pristine room. Warm wood tones buffer the highly contrasting neutrals of white and black, while brighter accessories in analogous blue and green are colorful but not overpowering. Verticality is accented with the tall clock that continues the rhythm of shadows in folds of the drapery. (Victoria Hagan)

Previous spread: Interiors in whites and black, like Zen black-and-white ink paintings, provide a tranquil retreat from chaotic modern life. Reflective exterior building materials of steel and glass are appropriated indoors for use in furniture and accessories. Windows frame urban views by day; at night they darken to balance the large dark paintings on opposite walls. (Gary Lee).

Above: Accents of black in circular, square, and rectangular form connect the floor and wall planes in this all-white room touched with just a hint of color. Softer, more traditional furniture and accessories provide comfort and complement the geometry. (Vicente Wolf)

the size of the room—but high ceilings in poorly proportioned rooms also present a challenge.

A simple value-study sketch can show how positive elements—the furniture, artwork, and accessories—by their shape and placement create negative space or shapes around them. Making a black-and-white copy of a color picture of a room can show how values are distributed, such as how values of the walls relate to the values in furniture and flooring. Medium to dark values are best done in planes; if used only in small dark accents—for example, in a highly contrasting picture frame, drapery rod, or molding—they can create a ribbon effect, and scattered dark accents can look like confetti.

As with all tonal values, the proportion and placement of light and dark fabrics and surfaces in a room are important considerations. When dealing with furniture, the contrast of a light-colored fabric on a traditional sofa that has an ornate, dark wood frame will focus attention on its graceful lines and details. On the other hand, a light color on upholstered seats of dining chairs that have dark frames can look like a series of squares and completely overshadow the frames. A piano or dark sofa can appear to levitate on a very light floor. Contrast also affects horizontal and vertical elements. It is best to avoid placing all dark values at a horizontal or sofa level and all light ones above at a vertical level. They should be distributed on both levels, with intermediate values to connect the two.

Balancing and Relating Horizontals to Verticals

Color cannot be separated from form. Just as a painting is a combination of color, value, texture, geometric composition, movement, and rhythm, the contents of a room should also be looked at in terms of these elements. Furniture should be seen as geometric shapes: the sofa, a horizontal rectangle; the bookcase, a vertical one; the table, a circle or square. The designer should think in terms of balancing voids with solids and relating horizontals—what is on the floor, or low furniture—to verticals— what is on the walls—in both color and tonal value. For example, a fireplace opening is in shadow; something medium to dark above the mantle will connect the two darker values to create a vertical. Placing a painting that has some darker values over a dark sofa or cabinet can bring the eye upward to connect the furniture to the art. A vertical bookcase can balance a door opening. This relationship can also extend into the room. An antique Venetian mirror with a silvery glass frame on a wall can relate to the sparkle of a crystal chandelier in the center of the room.

Balance can be found in relating colors on walls or draperies in some way to colors on the floor, as well as to furniture and accessories, in order to establish visual connections. If a sofa is seen against draperies, is there contrast and harmony of color and value? If a print is on one side of room, is it balanced elsewhere in color, pattern, and texture? The counterparts do not have to be identical in color: red fabric can be balanced by warm-colored wood such as mahogany, and a geometric pattern or stripe that has some of the drapery colors can be carried over to upholstered pieces. Balance can be achieved with artwork, books, and accessories in addition to fabric. A black piano does not have to be balanced by black—this would look too matched; balance is better achieved with a large item in dark blue.

Color and Concept

A successful color scheme is based on a sound concept, a step beyond merely assembling and matching colors and making arbitrary choices. Inspiration can come from many sources. As discussed in previous chapters, history, art, and nature serve as worthy guides, but the interpretation must be personal as well as somewhat abstract in order to avoid a cartoon effect. Will there be contemporary openness and transparency or Byzantine mystery? Radiant Vermeer lights or foggy mists? A dark room can be given light in different ways—the cool iridescence of a pearl with grays and light pastels, or the golden wash of sunset with reds.

Will a small room be turned into a comfortable retreat with medium to dark colors, breaking the rule that dictates it should have light colors to make it appear larger? Will the overall character be formal, informal, practical, or casual? Will it be fresh and crisp, or look aged, with the warm patina of worn leather, antique carpets, and crumbling paint? Will there be organized discipline or controlled chaos? Color decisions become easier and less arbitrary if based on a concept rather than imitation or formula.

Assembling the Color Scheme

In pulling together a color scheme, the first question invariably asked is, "Where do I begin?" The first considerations are the architecture and orientation of the room and the existing finishes, furniture, or art that have to remain. In the absence of these, one may begin with selecting items that are unique or more difficult to obtain: an antique carpet, a work of art, or natural material such as marble or wood. These are selected early in the process because there is a wide selection of fabric and paints available to coordinate with them; the reverse order can be much more difficult to accomplish.

A more mellow sense of tranquility can be achieved in neutral rooms in which medium and darker values predominate. The warmth of the reddish brown cabinet and gold picture frame is offset by the cooler taupe of the walls and draperies as well as by off-whites. The lightest values here create a vertical movement from the floor to the chair cushion, to the candles and painting. (Jackye Lanham)

In planning, it is best to consider the largest areas first: floor, walls, and major pieces of furniture. Too often people fall into the "pillow" or "footstool" syndrome—choosing a pleasing fabric for the smallest item and working outward to larger ones—and wind up in frustration.

Just as colors change in their juxtaposition to each other and under different lighting conditions, tastes change, for better or worse. Some rooms designed ten or twenty years ago appear fresh and current, while others, even more recent, look trendy or dated. Some show a superficial approach to color; others exhibit layers of understanding color, not in isolation but in combining form, pattern, texture, and light with panache. In addition to using history and nature as guides to understanding color, the designer should analyze color in a traditional or contemporary room in all its aspects. Is it monochromatic, analogous, complementary, or another scheme? What are the tonal variations? How are color and value distributed around the room? Are there prints, patterns, and textures? Are colors bright or more neutral? What are the proportions of white, black, and other neutrals? What is the positive/negative or ground/foreground relationship? Are architectural elements highlighted or are furniture and finishes more prominent? Rather than force old rules to new situations, one should rethink ways to interpret them. Drawing simple, loose renderings in watercolor or colored pencils and markers can help visualize a planned scheme.

A stumbling block in making decisions is inflexibility. Prematurely assigning a favorite fabric to a specific piece of furniture can result in a time-consuming process to coordinate the remaining fabrics. It is often easier to coordinate a favorite fabric with other fabrics and finishes, and then make assignments to furniture and drapery based on the layout of a room.

There is a tendency to develop a color scheme using primarily fabrics, or a combination of fabrics and paint samples, while ignoring other finishes that have color and value: wood floors and furniture, metal, glass, art, and accessories. Color schemes are mistakenly viewed in isolation rather than in their relationship to architectural finishes, which can be a large part of the room's surfaces. Keep in mind that the proportion of each color in a total scheme is important. Simply changing from a dark to a light wood floor can change the look of a fabric scheme; each substitution can have a domino effect and may require further changes. At this point, visual judgment should be used: one must observe, evaluate, analyze, decide, accept, or reject.

Samples should be looked at against a neutral background. Some designers prefer neutral gray, but white is often a better choice since it most often represents a large area of a room, such as the ceiling or walls. Samples of materials and finishes should be included even if they are white; subtle tints will be more distinct against a pure white background. Be conscious of reflection from surrounding walls or the exterior, as light can visually alter the surface color. Always evaluate large samples of finishes for major areas, such as walls and floors, and fabrics for draperies and large upholstered furniture. Look at these large samples from a distance, as small patterns and textures can mesh into solid colors or mix optically. In the gathered folds of drapery, fabric will take on a different look and a pattern will become compressed and darker than if it lies flat on a sofa.

Patterns and Prints

In dealing with patterns or prints to be used in major areas, begin by studying the wallcovering, carpet, or fabric. Are the colors complementary or analogous, many or few, warm or cool? What is the balance of color to neutrals, the value and chromatic range? Is the fabric traditional, contemporary, formal, or informal? Be selective when pulling colors out of a multicolor print and work with a major color or two, not accent colors, which are likely to disappear at a distance. Never try to match colors exactly to fabric in a room; color can be more effective when it is lighter or darker, less chromatic on walls and more so on smaller items. Keep in mind that a bright color next to a dull one will heighten their difference unless an intermediate range of chromatic and tonal values is used.

Optical mix is the effect in which several colors intertwine to give the impression of an overall color, rather than the actual individual colors. Instead of following the natural inclination to try to match colors in a patterned fabric exactly when coordinating it with other materials, remember that the eye mixes colors visually—for example, trying to match a blue and a green from a pattern will be less successful than using a blue-green that is not in the fabric but is more pleasing. This is especially true when selecting trim colors for marble, which may have many colors and tonal variations. The eye is blending all the colors; the correct color for coordination may be one that does not match a specific color in the marble but captures a visual mixture of all. Look at everything at a distance and as it will be when installed—carpet, horizontally on the floor, or paint and wallpaper vertically on walls—to see where textures or very small patterns may disappear. Remember to view schemes under both daylight and artificial light.

The wall color to accompany a patterned drapery can be taken from the background color of the print or from one of the more prominent colors, or be a tonal/chromatic variation of one of the colors. Bold prints against light walls will push the print forward; a medium value will provide a better balance. In relating textiles to other finishes in the room, a drapery pattern with primarily red-blue-green colors can relate on a horizontal level to a carpet that has a neutral ground, perhaps with red as a secondary color and a touch of darker blue to act as a grounding factor.

The color wheel provides a useful guide to finding the missing link if something seems to be lacking in a scheme. If a fabric has only one or two colors, look to analogous or complementary colors to add others to the scheme. These can be in other textiles, a carpet, or artwork that has the original color of the fabric and also introduces new ones. If red is the predominant color in a room and green secondary, the green can be varied among accents or accessories in an analogous way: blue-green to green to yellow-green.

A room should ideally have a balance of warm and cool colors, and other materials—glass, metals, marble, crystal, porcelain, art—also need to be evaluated in these terms. To achieve balance, it is better not to match all woods in furniture and flooring. Red or yellow walls can work better with cool brown wood floors rather than warmer browns. Warm woods usually work better with cool colored walls. If walls are blue, warm wood tones are really a neutralized orange, the complement of blue.

Rooms that are highly colored need some white, or very light neutrals, for a "breath of fresh air," as well as to provide a background for darker colors. The neutrals serve as a backdrop or contrast so the color can be appreciated and visual fatigue can be avoided by providing a resting place for the eyes. Just as an all-white room can be disturbing to some, too much color can be fatiguing as well.

Three colors (or other odd numbers) work better than two. In a one-color fabric such as a blue toile, there is the need for the warmth of yellow and warm woods to surround it. Create a neutral if one does not exist in a print: browns in warm colors, grays in cool colors, which can be coordinated or contrasted with the original color. Pull in colors from the print around the room—in artwork, other fabrics, carpet, screens—in different values and proportions. Another general rule when using colors together—especially in large areas—is to change the value if the color changes; a dark blue may look better next to a lighter green than a dark green. When choosing the color for a fringe to be added to a multi-color print on a sofa or large chair, it's usually better to lean toward the darker colors in the fabric in order to ground the piece; a darker, plain fabric can have a lighter fringe provided there is not too great a contrast.

Geometric patterns are a good mix with floral prints and texture if there is some relationship among colors and the scale is right.[6] Coloring in prints can be heavy or light, vivid or low in chroma. Very dark or very light or bright solid fabrics on large, bulky furniture may add to their bulk or be overbearing.

---

6. This concept is successfully carried out in the Japanese kimono shown on p. 75.

In upholstered pieces, colors in the ground or foreground of a floral fabric make a difference. Fabric with a light background can have a delicacy that may contradict the bulk of a sofa; a darker background would be preferable. Colors should be in balance around a room but do not have to be the same. Too much harmony can be boring. In fine art, a painting often has a color that is a little out of place, but without which the painting is bland.

The quality of paint colors in large areas such as walls is important and should ideally contain the full spectrum. Note that paint or fabric that looks fresh and crisp will make antique carpets or textiles look dirty, so the chromatic level will need to be adjusted. Marble needs fabric that has sparkle rather than drabness, and the fabric in turn needs to be seen against walls with some texture or chromatic interest.

Wallpaper

Historically, scenic wallpapers have been used successfully in halls and dining rooms. In the case of large-scaled or scenic wallpapers, keep in mind doors or other openings that will interrupt the scene, as well as ceiling height. More vivid colors can be used in hallways, powder rooms, and other transitional spaces. If there is a dado, be sure the paint colors selected to accompany the wallpaper are similar in value and intensity to the wallpaper, as an abrupt change will cut the room in half. The major emphasis should be on color and form, not on color alone. Keep in mind that wallpaper is usually a difficult background for art, because its pattern competes with the artwork.

Throughout history, the study of different cultures or previous periods has inspired succeeding generations not to copy but to move onward to create new interpretations. The study of color and its application to interiors, traditional or modern, is best approached in this spirit. It is based on observation of nature and knowledge of the fine and decorative arts along with a visual and analytical approach as to why styles and colors work or don't work.

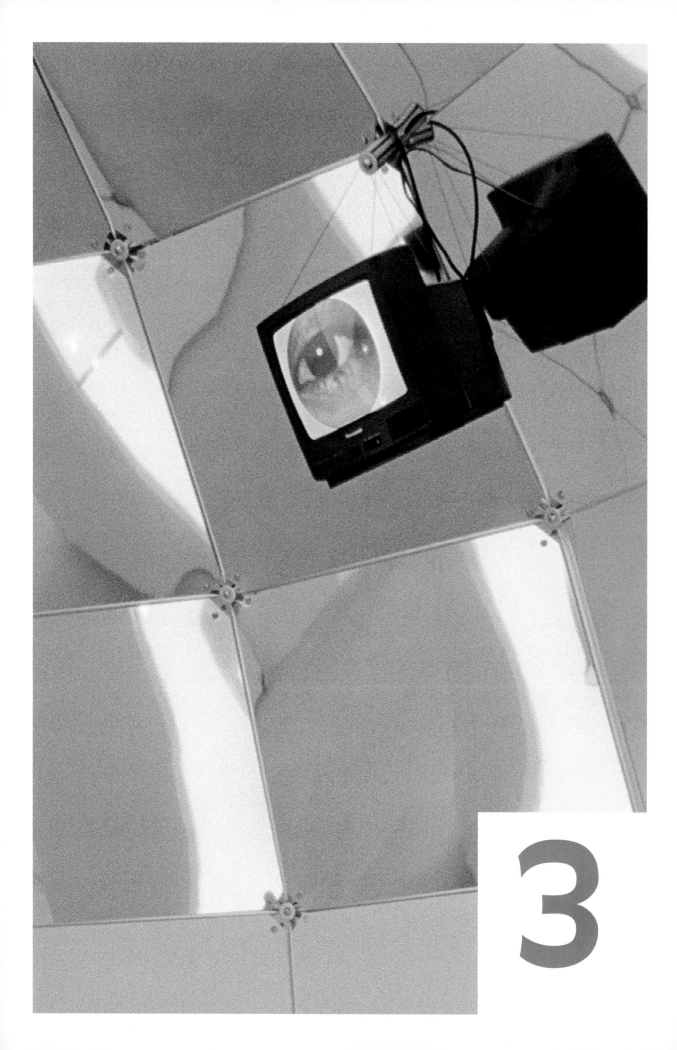

3

IT IS HARD TO BELIEVE that interiors we look upon today as modern—those designed by Mies van der Rohe, Le Corbusier, and Chareau, for example—are almost eighty years old and still look fresh and timeless. Traditional rooms dating back to eighteenth-century England and France are still copied on a smaller scale and modified to meet today's aesthetic. A survey of home furnishings magazines over the past ten years will show that some rooms have remained fresh and appealing, while others appear trendy or outdated. Further analysis of the less enduring ones typically reveals a lack of attention to scale and proportion; a poor understanding of color, value, and texture; or the clutter of superfluous accessories in an attempt to camouflage design or color short-comings—all issues raised by Edith Wharton in *The Decoration of Houses* in 1897.

Elsie De Wolfe is considered the first American woman to become a professional decorator, starting with her design of the Colony Club in New York City in 1905. Bowing to the credo of Wharton and Codman, De Wolfe adhered to a motto of "simplicity, suitability, and proportion," and published her own book, *The House in Good Taste*, in 1913. Moving beyond tradition, however, she created an eclectic interior in her home in France, the Villa Trianon in Versailles. She mixed antiques with contemporary furniture and combined a soft eighteenth-century palette of muted rose, blues, and grays with bold stripes and leopard-print fabrics. After moving to California in her later years, she daringly covered her walls with green lacquer.[1]

Designers and decorators in the 1920s, '30s, and '40s inspired by the Bauhaus, Ballets Russes, and new art movements, were to raise the bar on innovation in many different directions. In 1922, while Paris was still under the spell of bright, Scheher-azade colors, fashion designer Coco Chanel made a startling impression by opening her beige Paris salon. Ruhlmann also designed interiors in primarily neutral palettes of beiges and browns for private clients. The pendulum swung back in 1930, when Van Gogh's sunflowers in bursts of yellow and green at an exhibit in New York's Museum of Modern Art had the same effect as had the ballet in influencing color in both fashion and home furnishings. Surrealist art was the influence for fashion designer Elsa Schaparelli, who used bold colors that led to "shocking" pink in the late 1930s; this color, along with bright yellows and greens, would later filter into American interiors.[2]

London decorator Syrie Maugham and French decorator and furniture designer Jean-Michel Frank straddled both the trend of all neutral and the popularity of bold color. Maugham is thought to be one of the first to champion the all-white room, trying it out on her own living room in 1927 before doing many for her clients. Its fresh appeal came from her use of a variety of tinted whites as well as a contrast of textures to create

The Revolving Door of Color Trends

Page 198: Detail of "Spaced Out" (see p. 206)

Above: An antidote to overcast skies in London is the sunny yellow drawing room designed by American Nancy Lancaster in collaboration with English decorator John Fowler.

depth. A theatrical touch was provided by indirect lighting and mirrors that scattered reflections. After the white trend declined in 1934, Maugham returned to the liberal use of color. Jean-Michel Frank, whose career was at its height in the 1930s, went from a beige and white palette with ebony for accent to the use of bright chintzes.[3]

Dorothy Draper, an American who specialized in hotel design in the 1930s and '40s, set the trend for large-scale floral chintz patterns in vivid pinks, reds, blues, and greens, often against a white background. Another American, Nancy Lancaster, went on to acquire the British design firm of Colefax & Fowler in 1946 and designed the famed yellow drawing room in the firm's London antique showroom in collaboration with John Fowler, who restored or redecorated many of England's great historic houses.

In America, a building boom in middle-class residential housing followed World War II, and manufacturers were quick to abandon practical grays and beiges and step in with new products and a greatly expanded palette of colors not only in paints but also in carpets, textiles, linens, leathers, plastic laminates, and appliances. In 1946, a leading home furnishings magazine, *House & Garden*, began conducting surveys among shoppers and designers to identify and respond to consumer needs and to spot emerging trends. A 1953 survey revealed that half of the respondents found color to be the most problematic in decorating; either they did not know how to use favorite colors, or they had difficulty in obtaining them in furnishings. Both issues were readily taken on by publishers and manufacturers.[4]

A feature article in the magazine the year before expressed awareness of the changing times and changing architecture:

Our Victorian ancestors felt impelled to accentuate the ornate heaviness of their living rooms with a rich and somber palette. Today, we complement the structural airiness of our new homes with light, bright colors, distinct enough to compete with the view beyond the picture window. This change in attitude is influenced by the change in architecture. It is also determined by the tempo of our lives. We move faster than our grandparents did, we cover more ground. Their parlors bristled with objects, implying that they had the leisure to enjoy them. Ours are stripped by comparison; we use color broadly, as though to catch the eye on the run. This is the new way with color—a forthright way that frankly does double-duty in replacing ornamentation.[5]

The article went on to introduce bright new pastels, but there were no apparent rules or guidelines, natural or historic, for the application of these colors. While nature

1. Suzanne Trocmé, *Influential Interiors*, 62.
2. Donald Pavey et al., *Colour*, 120.
3. *Influential Interiors*, 63, 65.
4. *House & Garden*, "Good Colors Add Up To Good Living," Sept. 1953, 106.
5. Ibid, "The New Way with Color," Sept. 1952, 80.

reserves the brightest colors for smaller accents, the new bright colors were often unleashed with abandon on large areas of the room—walls, floor, and furniture.

Early 1950s rooms presented a seesaw variation in color: in some rooms, the earth-toned schemes reminiscent of Frank Lloyd Wright with beige, terra cotta, orange, and brown predominated; other rooms vibrated with the bright new pastels. Although many of these rooms would be unsettling to our whitewashed eyes today, they provided a much-needed emotional lift after the drab and depressing years of war.

The homeowner was advised to paint the walls and ceiling of a small room with one pastel color to make it seem larger; for large rooms the advice was to paint one wall a bright color, such as orange, and keep the other walls neutral. Many featured rooms were monochromatic—for example, an all-blue living room or an all-green dining room—or in a spectrum of one color, such as a pink-red-mauve living room. In some rooms there was overbearing use of a single color with few neutrals or complementary touches offered for relief. Nature's distribution was upset as well—a large "Siamese" (formerly "shocking") pink area rug underfoot where one would expect the more muted tones of earth.

A complementary scheme was introduced as the "watermelon look," pink and green with small black accents. Not limited to living room or bedroom, the scheme was carried into a kitchen advertisement that showed a green floor and pink laminate cabinets. Although the appliances were still white, color soon spread to stoves and refrigerators.

Patterns were not predominant in 1950s style. Even area rugs were solid colors, making them more striking. The trend of a one- or two-color scheme with a few neutrals continued through the decade: red-white-brown; green-purple-white; pink-blue-white; and black-white-turquoise with yellow-green, among others. Pink and green remained fashionable over the years, appearing on a magazine cover even in the late 1970s. The combination still occasionally surfaces today in the pink and green bathroom fixtures and tile of unrenovated houses.

Patterns and textures were more evident in the 1960s, and color remained strong. White or neutral walls were commonly seen, providing strong contrast with the colors in furnishings such as orange and gold or orange with green. Red, white, and blue combinations emerged, and greens were still popular, mixed together in analogous schemes ranging from yellow to blue-greens, like a salad with bits of red, orange, and yellow for accent. The room with a single brightly painted wall remained, but with the addition of graphics on the walls, waves of orange and blue or stripes in all colors of the spectrum. White shag area rugs now provided both texture and

Rooms with one brightly colored wall were common in the 1950s.
The George Eastman House, Rochester, New York.

neutral relief. Room schemes varied from almost neutral palettes to mixtures of too many colors.

The mid-1960s saw a shift to softer pastels and more neutrals and white walls with bright colors reserved for accents. One scheme was ahead of its time: a room in almost all white and putty colors with browns to near-black in a good value range. It would be perfectly livable today if the overabundant of green plants were removed. Other neutral rooms featured orange and black accents. Later in the decade, a more sophisticated attention to value as well as color was evident in a room with white walls, black floor, zebra area rug, and a bright red/blue/green scheme in the art and accents. Pink and green were still strong, but yellow was added to balance the spectrum and take away the sweetness. Toward the end of the '60s, harvest gold and avocado green began their domination in home furnishings to the point that the colors became almost intolerable a decade later.

The 1970s featured more rooms with white walls and bright color accents and more beige/brown/black combined with colors. Fabrics appeared in large-scale prints and bold colors. In this decade, rooms varied from those having white or neutral walls and floors with color accents in furniture and accessories to rooms where white sofas contrasted with vibrant red, orange, green, or blue walls. Soft pastels of pink and blue could be combined with strong red and brown, as in a room with chocolate brown walls and pink draperies, while other rooms disagreeably combined too many colors and patterns resulting in a dollhouse look. Orange, brown, and white or beige were still a popular combination. At the same time there were neutral rooms where texture and form minimized or replaced color: one with a modified "Japanese look"; another, all white and brown in a range of values with no color or clutter such as pillows or plants. The browns of furniture and accessories provided highly contrasting sculptural forms against white walls and floors. Ceilings were occasionally painted—a red-walled living room and a green-walled dining room, both with sky blue ceilings. The serenity of neutrals versus the seduction of color continued, with variations, through the end of the twentieth century.

Design in the new twenty-first century appears to be at a crossroads similar to that of Victorian times. Instead of the challenges and controversies of moving from hand-crafts to the machine, we have moved beyond the machine to ever-present electronic technologies. In Victorian times, machine-made products were a poor imitation of previous styles until faculty and students at the Bauhaus took a fresh approach to using the machine and new materials to create innovative designs. In the digital age, the emphasis is still on consumerism, but, in spite of many more choices in colors and products, no distinctly new styles have emerged.

The twenty-first century equivalent of Victorian clutter in interiors is, to some degree, the visual clutter of the often harsh colors of commercial products and packaging, print graphics, and the moving images on television screens and computers. Colors that are eye-catching and successful in merchandising may not be livable color schemes in interiors. After shifting between opposite poles of color and no color over the last few decades, designers for the most part have wiped the slate clean and reverted to all-white or beige rooms. This is not necessarily bad; well-designed neutral rooms can be beautiful and refined, and a much-needed therapeutic solution to too many distractions and the assault of commercial color. The downside to a room devoid of color and texture is that, though it may photograph well, in the law of contrasts anything needed for simple living—a newspaper or a coffee cup—is magnified and can upset the perfection. This may perfectly suit some clients, while others prefer rooms with color and pattern where some day-to-day clutter does not appear too untidy.

A trend toward minimalism has not decreased the need for flamboyance. The sparkle of gold and ormolu is expressed in modern ways with shiny metals, metallics, and pearlized finishes, and iridescent or transparent fabrics threaded with glitter or gems. The polished marble, mirrors, and lights of Versailles have been retained to continue giving a sense of luxury, to expand small spaces, and to create moods. A 1968 interior featured stretch-fabric wall panels washed with changing tinted lights; the idea was ahead of its time and has reemerged in commercial spaces as well as homes. Colors projected on walls with lights provide a new way of applying color that can be changed instantly for theatrical effects and require no paint mixing or patience.

We seem to be in a revolving door between traditional and modern styles: one foot in the past, the other in the future. There are valid reasons for both traditional and modern styles, and both can be creatively mixed. Seventeenth- and eighteenth-century architect/designers borrowed ideas from past cultures, reinterpreted them, and combined them with elegance and style. Furniture crossed generations, and periods were mixed together creatively to blend with the interior architecture. New images of the future are emerging, but only time will tell if they are mere trends.

The color pendulum still swings back and forth, from little or no color to too much color, often with more whimsy than wisdom. In its suppression of ornament, modern architecture seems to have suppressed color, although some architects like Le Corbusier, also an artist, applied it to interiors. Our continued use of and pleasure in the past may

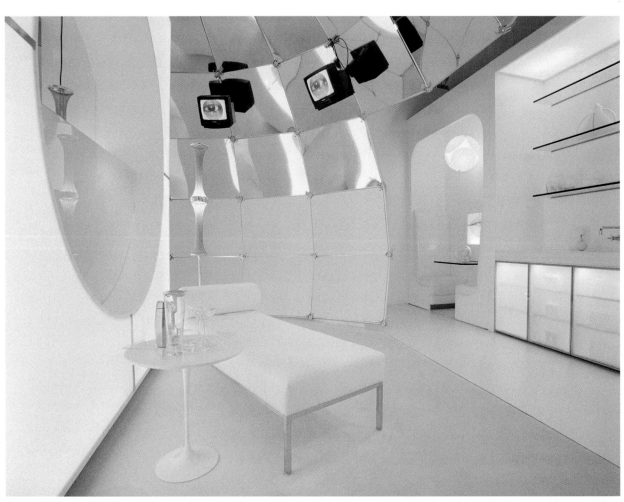

be, in a way, a subliminal search for color and texture, to which tradition is more hospitable. Historic interiors brought the vivid colors and textures of nature indoors; this has been exchanged for subdued interiors with outdoor views, natural or urban.

Color can work in modern interiors, and there are currently occasional pockets of revolution among the color-starved, such as the youthful revival of the flamboyant 1960s style of British decorator David Hicks. We still too often think of color in terms of the primaries and secondaries of childhood instead of its more subtle yet energetic nuances. Color does not have to be bold. One can ease from white, which if too stark will hurt the eyes, to pale grays, taupes, or neutralized tints that, with careful pigment mixture, are not drab. Think of natural materials, such as stone or limestone, shells and sand, neutrals with mixtures of many colors. More pronounced color can still be used, but with discretion on freestanding walls, recessed wall planes, or other accent areas. Designers are challenged by large wall areas of contemporary rooms with cathedral ceilings and no division to break down the scale. Color on these large surfaces could be overwhelming, but the serenity of off-white can be maintained while adding a wash of color with a large, near-monochromatic painting or screen.

One constant throughout history has been the human need for not only color but also change and variety. A study of artists and designers of the past also reveals the need for individual change and growth as part of creativity. Designers can test new ideas in either their own homes or in public show houses where client strictures can be set aside, and radical ideas often turn into interesting new trends. There are many choices in living styles; the solution must be personal. For color inspiration, either moving outward or withdrawing inward are sustainable—both nature and fine art have withstood the test of time.

We are now, as ever, adapting to change and new technologies, but beauty is still a highly valued pursuit, and color will always play a vital role. Color should not be approached superficially. It needs to be nourished with a constant study of art, history, and nature to stimulate the creative imagination and, with a restraint that comes with knowledge, to forge on to new interpretations.

Opposite, above: "Spaced Out," a futuristic concept from an interior design show in Toronto in 2001. The space is a hygienic, compact capsule for living, dining, and food preparation.

Opposite, below: Nature and technology compete for attention in this contemporary bedroom. Paneled and frescoed walls of the past are replaced by exterior views, which have become part of the interior through glass and steel construction, along with images of the world through the wide-screen television. Both provide changing scenes and a medium for serenity or drama. (Holger Schubert)

Abercrombie, Stanley. "Lincoln's Inn Fields." *Interior Design* Magazine, July 1985.

——. "Palazzo Davanzati." *Interior Design* Magazine, March 1988.

Ackerman, James S. *The Villa, Form and Ideology of Country Houses.* The A.W. Mellon Lectures in the Fine Arts, 1985, The National Gallery of Art, Washington, D.C. Bollingen Series XXXV.34. Princeton, NJ.: Princeton University Press, 1990.

Adams, William Howard. *Jefferson's Monticello.* New York: Abbeville Press, 1983.

Albers, Josef. *Interaction of Color.* New Haven and London: Yale University Press, 1963.

Anderson, Maxwell L. *Pompeian Frescoes in The Metropolitan Museum of Art.* The Metropolitan Museum of Art Bulletin, Winter 1987/88.

Ardalan, Nader, and Laleh Bakhtiar. *The Sense of Unity, The Sufi Tradition in Persian Architecture.* Chicago and London: The University of Chicago Press, 1973.

Arieti, Silvano. *Creativity, The Magic Synthesis.* New York: Basic Books, Inc., Harper Colophon Books, 1976.

Bartlett, John. *Bartlett's Familiar Quotations*, 16th ed. Edited by Justin Kaplan. Toronto, London: Little, Brown and Company, 1992.

Battersby, Martin. *The Triumph of Style: Art Deco. The History of Furniture.* New York: William Morrow & Company, Inc., 1976.

Bauer, Jaroslav. *Minerals, Rocks and Precious Stones.* London: Treasure Press, 1992.

Birren, Faber. *Color & Human Response.* New York: Van Nostrand Reinhold Company, Inc., 1978.

——. *Color for Interiors, Historical and Modern.* New York: Whitney Library of Design, 1963.

——. *Color, A Survey in Words and Pictures.* Secaucus, NJ.: Citadel Press, 1963.

——. *The Power of Color,* A Citadel Press Book. Secaucus, NJ: Carol Publishing Group, 1997.

——. *Principles of Color, A Review of Past Tradition & Modern Theories.* New York: Van Nostrand Reinhold Company, Inc., 1969.

Calloway, Stephen, and Elizabeth Cromley. *The Elements of Style.* New York: Simon and Schuster, 1991.

Camard, Florence. *Ruhlmann, Master of Art Deco.* Translated by David Macey. New York: Harry N. Abrams, Inc., 1984.

Cantor, Jay E. *Winterthur.* New York: Harry N. Abrams, Inc., 1997.

Chevreul, M.E. *The Principles of Harmony and Contrast of Colors.* Introduction & Commentary by Faber Birren. West Chester, PA: Schiffer Publishing Co., 1987.

Ching, Francis D.K. *Interior Design Illustrated.* New York: Van Nostrand Reinhold Company, Inc., 1987.

Classic American Homes. "The Ballantine House Library: Reading Red." Holiday 2000.

Colby, Barbara. *Color & Light: Influences and Impact.* Glendale, CA: Chroma Productions, 1990.

Cole, Bruce. *Giotto: The Scrovegni Chapel, Padua.* New York: George Braziller, Inc., 1993.

Colman, David. "Summoning a 60's Ghost: It's Groovy, Baby." *New York Times*, March 6, 2003.

Color Symbolism. Six excerpts from the Eranos yearbook, 1972. Huyghe, René: *Color and the Expression of Interior Time in Western Art;* Izutsu, Toshihiko: *The Elimination of Colour in Far Eastern Art and Philosophy;* Rowe, Christopher: *Concepts of Colour and Colour Symbolism in the Ancient World;* Zahan, Dominique: *White, Red and Black: Colour Symbolism in Black Africa.* Dallas: Spring Publications, Inc. 1994.

Connaissance des Arts. Fontainebleau. Paris: SFPA 1991.

Cook, Olive. *The English Country House.* New York: G.P. Putnam's Sons, 1974.

——. *The English House Through Seven Centuries.* Woodstock, N.Y.: The Overlook Press, 1983.

Cooper, Jeremy. *Victorian and Edwardian Decor.* New York: Abbeville Press, 1987.

Craig, Theresa. *Edith Wharton, A House Full of Rooms: Architecture, Interiors, and Gardens.* New York: The Monacelli Press, 1996.

Curatola, Giovanni. *The Simon and Schuster Book of Oriental Carpets.* Translated by Arnoldo Mondadori. New York: Simon and Schuster, 1982.

Davaras, Costis. *The Palace of Knossos.* Athens: Editions Hannibal, n.d.

David, A. Rosalie. *The Egyptian Kingdoms.* New York: Elsevier Phaidon, 1975.

Davidson, Marshall B., and Elizabeth Stillinger. *The American Wing at The Metropolitan Museum of Art.* New York: Alfred A. Knopf, 1985.

De la Croix, Horst, and Richard G. Tansey. *Gardner's Art Through the Ages.* 7th ed. New York: Harcourt Brace Janovich, Inc. 1980.

BIBLIOGRAPHY

Delamare, François, and Bernard Guineau. *Colors, The Story of Dyes and Pigments*. Translated by Sophie Hawkes. New York: Discoveries, Harry N. Abrams, Inc., 2000.

Dion-Tennenbaum, Anne. *The Great Jacob. Beaux Arts, Decorative Arts 1799–1814*. Paris: Beaux Arts Magazine, 1992.

Dresser, Christopher. *Principles of Victorian Decorative Design*. Mineola, NY: Dover Publications, Inc., 1995. An unabridged replication of "Principles of Decorative Design," 2nd edition, published by Cassell Petter & Galpin, London.

Duquette, Tony. "Design Classics—Elsie de Wolfe." *Architectural Digest*, n.d.

Durant, Will. *The Life of Greece, The Story of Civilization II*. New York: Simon and Schuster, 1966.

——. *Caesar and Christ, The Story of Civilization III*. New York: Simon and Schuster, 1944.

——. *The Age of Faith, The Story of Civilization IV*. New York: Simon and Schuster, 1950.

——. *The Renaissance, The Story of Civilization V*. New York: Simon and Schuster, 1953.

Durant, Will, and Ariel Durant. *The Age of Louis XIV. The Story of Civilization VIII*. New York: Simon and Schuster, 1963.

——. *Rousseau and Revolution. The Story of Civilization X*. New York: Simon and Schuster, 1967.

Edwards, I.E.S. *Tutankhamun: His Tomb and Its Treasures*. New York: The Metropolitan Museum of Art and Alfred A. Knopf, Inc., 1978.

Emerson, Ralph Waldo. *Essays by Ralph Waldo Emerson*. The World's Greatest Literature. London: The Spencer Press, 1936.

Erlande-Brandenburg, Alain. *The Lady and the Unicorn*. Paris: Editions de la Réunion des musées nationaux, 1989.

Escritt, Stephen. *Art Nouveau*. London: Phaidon Press Ltd., 2000.

Fagan, Bryan. *Egypt of the Pharoahs*. Washington, D.C.: National Geographic Society, 2001.

Fahr-Becker, Gabriele. *Art Nouveau*. Cologne: Könemann, 1997.

Farnoux, Alexandre. *Knossos, Searching for the Legendary Palace of King Minos*. New York: Discoveries, Harry N. Abrams, Inc., 1996.

Feisner, Edith Anderson. *Color Studies*. New York: Fairchild Publications, Inc., 2001.

Feller, Robert L., and Charles Parkhurst. *Color Research and Application*. Vol. 7, No. 3, Fall 1982. "Who Invented the Color Wheel?" Presented at the ISCC Color Conference 1981. New York: John Wiley & Sons, Inc.

Finlay, Victoria. *Colour—Travels Through the Paint Box*. London: Hodder and Stoughton Div. of Hodder Headline, 2002.

Frampton, Kenneth. *Le Corbusier, Architect of the Twentieth Century*. New York: Harry N. Abrams, Inc., 2002.

——. *Modern Architecture, A Critical History*. New York and Toronto: Oxford University Press, 1980.

Freeman, Margaret B. *The Unicorn Tapestries*. Adaptation by Linda Sipress. The Metropolitan Museum of Art Bulletin No. 1, 1973/1974.

Frelinghuysen, Alice Cooney. *Louis Comfort Tiffany at The Metropolitan Museum of Art*. The Metropolitan Museum of Art Bulletin, Summer 1998.

Fremantle, Richard. *Masaccio*. New York: Smithmark Publishers, 1998.

Friedman, Joe. *Inside Paris*. London: Phaidon Press Ltd., 1989.

Friedman, Joseph. English Translation. *Vaux-Le-Vicomte*. France: Publications-Elysees, n.d.

Gage, John. *Color and Culture*. Boston, Toronto, London: A Bulfinch Press Book; Little, Brown and Company, 1993.

——. *Color and Meaning: Art, Science, and Symbolism*. Berkeley and Los Angeles: University of California Press, 1999.

Gale, Iain, and Richard Bryant. *Living Museums*. Boston: A Bulfinch Press Book, Little, Brown and Company, 1993.

Gardiner, Stephen. *Le Corbusier*. Edited by Frank Kermode. New York: The Viking Press, 1974.

Garrett, Wendell. *American Colonial, Puritan Simplicity to Georgian Grace*. New York: The Monacelli Press, 1995.

——. *Classic America, The Federal Style and Beyond*. New York: Universe Publishing, 1995.

Gilliatt, Mary. *Period Style*. Boston, Toronto, London: Little, Brown and Company, 1990.

Ginsburg, Madeleine, ed. *The Illustrated History of Textiles*. London: Studio Editions Ltd., 1993.

Goethe, Johann Wolfgang von. *Theory of Colours*. Translated by Charles Lock Eastlake. Cambridge, MA and London: The M.I.T. Press, 2000.

Page 208: Detail, the Davanzati Palace, Florence (see p. 22).

Graves, Maitland E. *Color Fundamentals*. New York: McGraw Hill, 1952.

Gowing, Lawrence. *Paintings in the Louvre*. New York: Stewart, Tabori & Chang, 1987.

Grow, Lawrence, and Dina von Zweck. *American Victorian*. New York: Perennial Library, 1985.

Halén, Widar. *Christopher Dresser*. London: Phaidon Press Limited, 1993.

Harris, William H., and Judith S. Levy, eds. *The New Columbia Encyclopedia*. New York and London: Columbia University Press, 1975.

Hayward, Helena, ed. *World Furniture*. Secaucus, N.J.: Chartwell Books, Inc., 1976.

Hitchcock, Henry-Russell. *The Pelican History of Art. Architecture: Nineteenth and Twentieth Centuries*. New York: Penguin Books, 1978.

Hoog, Simone, and Daniel Meyer. *Versailles, Complete Guide*. Translated by Bronia Fuchs-Willig. Versailles: Editions d'Art Lys, 1992.

Hope, Augustine, and Margaret Walch. *The Color Compendium*. New York: Van Nostrand Reinhold, 1990.

——. *Living Colors*. San Francisco: Chronicle Books, 1995.

Ilse-Neuman, Ursula. *Bauhaus Workshops, 1919–1933*. The American Craft Museum Exhibition Catalog. New York: Metropolis Magazine, 1994.

Innes, Jocasta. *Paint Magic*. New York: Pantheon Books, 1987.

Interiors & Sources Magazine. "The Six Ways That Humans Process Color." Oct. 2000.

Itten, Johannes. *The Art of Color*. Translated by Ernst van Hagen. New York: John Wiley & Sons, Inc.,1973.

——. *Design and Form*. New York: Van Nostrand Reinhold Company, Inc., 1975.

——. *The Elements of Color*. Edited by Faber Birren. Translated by Ernst van Hagen. New York: John Wiley & Sons, Inc., 2001.

Jackson-Stops, Gervase, and James Pipkin. *The English Country House, A Grand Tour*. New York Graphic Society and the National Gallery of Art, Washington, D.C., Boston and Toronto: Little, Brown and Company, 1985.

Jones, Anthony. *Charles Rennie Mackintosh*. London: Studio Editions, 1990.

Jones, Chester. *Colefax & Fowler, The Best in English Interior Decoration*. Boston, Toronto, London: A Bulfinch Press Book; Little, Brown and Company, 1989.

Jones, Owen. *The Grammar of Ornament*. London: A Dorling Kindersley Book, The Ivy Press Limited, 2001.

Kandinsky, Wassily. *Kandinsky, Complete Writings on Art*. Edited by Kenneth C. Lindsay and Peter Vergo. New York: Da Capo Press, Inc., 1994.

Kaufman, Donald, and Taffy Dahl. *Color and Light, Luminous Atmospheres for Painted Rooms*. Text by Christine Pittel. New York: Clarkson Potter/ Publishers, 1999.

——. *Color, Natural Palettes for Painted Rooms*. Text by Laurel Graeber. New York: Clarkson Potter Publishers, 1992.

Klein, Dan. *All Color Book of Art Deco*. London: Octopus Books Ltd., 1974.

Kramer, Jennifer. "The Legendary Nancy Lancaster." *Southern Accents* Magazine, March-April 2001.

Lampugnani, Vittorio Magnago, ed. *Encyclopedia of 20th Century Architecture*. New York: Harry N. Abrams, Inc., 1986.

Lee, Lawrence, George Seddon, and Francis Stephens. *Stained Glass*. New York: Crown Publishers, Inc., 1976.

Long, Jim, and Joy Turner Luke. *The New Munsell Student Color Set*. Second Edition. New York: Fairchild Publications Inc., 2001.

Lüscher, Max. *The Lüscher Color Test*. Translated and edited by Ian Scott. New York: Washington Square Press, Div. of Simon and Schuster, 1971.

"Malmaison." www.georgianindex.net /Napoleon/ Malmaison.malmaison.html, 2002.

Mang, Karl. *History of Modern Furniture*. Translated by John William Gabriel. New York: Harry N. Abrams, Inc., 1979.

Marasovič, Tomislav. *Diocletian's Palace*. Translated by Sonja Biačnič. Yugoslavia: Little Art Books, 1970.

Massie, Suzanne. *Land of the Firebird*. New York: Simon and Schuster, 1980.

Mathieu, Caroline. *Guide to the Musée d'Orsay*. Translated by Anthony Roberts. Paris: Edition de la Réunion des musées nationaux, 1992.

McAlester, Virginia and Lee. *Great American Houses and Their Architectural Styles*. New York: Abbeville Press, 1994.

Menten, Theodore. *The Art Deco Style.* New York: Dover
  Publications, 1972.

Miller, Judith. *Judith Miller's Color.* New York: Clarkson
  Potter Publishers, 2000.

Miller, Malcolm. *Chartres Cathedral.* Pitkin Guides. UK:
  Pitkin Unichrome, Ltd. 2001.

Mitchell, C. Thomas, and Jiangmei Wu. *Living Design:
  The Daoist Way of Building.* New York: McGraw-Hill,
  1998.

Moos, Stanislaus von, and Arthur Rüegg, eds. *Le
  Corbusier before Le Corbusier 1907–1922.* New York:
  Bard Graduate Center, and New Haven, CT: Yale
  University Press, 2002.

Morel-Journel, Guillemette. *Le Corbusier's Villa Savoye.*
  Translated by Mary Pardoe. Paris: Centres des
  monuments nationaux/Éditions du patrimoine,
  2000.

Morley-Fletcher, Hugo. *Techniques of the World's Great
  Masters of Pottery and Ceramics.* Edison, NJ:
  Chartwell Books, Inc., 1997.

Muraro, Michelangelo, and Paolo Marton. *Venetian
  Villas.* Cologne: Könemann, 1986.

Negus, Arthur. *A Tour of Twelve Great Country Houses.*
  London: Peerage Books, 1989.

New York School of Interior Design. *Color and Its Use in
  Interior Design and Decoration,* 1983.

Newhall, Beaumont. "Art: Fragments of History,
  Dramatic Statements in Black and White."
  Architectural Digest Magazine, n.d.

Nuckolls, James L. *Interior Lighting for Environmental
  Designers.* New York: John Wiley & Sons, 1976.

Ostwald, Wilhelm. *The Color Primer, A Basic Treatise on
  the Color System of Wilhelm Ostwald.* Edited by Faber
  Birren. New York: Van Nostrand Reinhold
  Company, Inc., 1969.

Pastoureau, Michel. *Blue, The History of a Color.*
  Translated by Markus I. Cruse. Princeton, NJ:
  Princeton University Press, 2001.

Patrick, Richard. *All Color Book of Egyptian Mythology.*
  London: Octopus Books Limited, 1972.

Patton, Phil. "Lost in Space: Living Room for the
  Crew." *New York Times,* Sept. 8, 1994.

Pavey, Donald, Madge Garland, Deryck Healey, John
  Gage, Faber Birren, Carl Foss, Yale Forman. *Colour.*
  London: Marshall Editions Ltd., Grange Books,
  1991.

Peck, Amelia. *The Frank Lloyd Wright Room. Period
  Rooms in The Metropolitan Museum of Art.* New York:
  Harry N. Abrams, Inc., 1996.

Pegler, Martin M. *The Dictionary of Interior Design.* New
  York: Fairchild Publications, 1983.

Pevsner, Nikolaus. *Pioneers of Modern Design.* New York:
  A Pelican Book, Penguin Books, 1975.

Porter, Tom. *Architectural Color.* New York: Whitney
  Library of Design, 1982.

Pumphrey, Richard. *Elements of Art.* Upper Saddle
  River, NJ: Prentice Hall, 1996.

Rief, Rita. *Treasure Rooms of America's Great Mansions.*
  Waukesha, WI: Country Beautiful, MCMLXX.

Riley, Terence, and Barry Bergdoll. *Mies in Berlin.* New
  York: The Museum of Modern Art, 2001.

Roberts-Jones, Philippe, ed. *Brussels, Fin de Siecle.*
  Translated by Sue Rose Wembley. Cologne:
  Evergreen, 1999.

Roth, Leland M. *A Concise History of American
  Architecture.* New York: Icon Editions, Harper &
  Row, 1980.

Ruskin, John. *The Stones of Venice.* Edited by J.G. Links.
  New York: Da Capo Press 1960.

Scully, Vincent. *Architecture, The Natural and the
  Manmade.* New York: St. Martin's Press 1991.

Sharpe, Deborah T. *The Psychology of Color and Design.*
  Totowa, NJ: Littlefield, Adams & Co., 1981.

Simon & Schuster's Guide to Rocks and Minerals. Edited
  by Martin Prinz et al. New York: Simon & Schuster,
  1978.

Snodin, Michael, and John Styles. *Design & The
  Decorative Arts, Britain 1500–1900.* London: V & A
  Publications, 2001.

Suplee, Curt. *Milestones of Science.* Washington, D.C.:
  National Geographic Society, 2000.

Tilton, John Kent. *A History of Color as Used in Textiles.*
  Long Island City, NY: Scalamandre Silks, Inc., n.d.

Trocmé, Suzanne. *Influential Interiors.* New York:
  Clarkson Potter Publishers, 1999.

Watkin, David. *A History of Western Architecture.* New
  York: Thames and Hudson, 1986.

Weber, Eva. *Art Deco in America.* New York: Exeter
  Books, 1985.

Webster's Seventh New Collegiate Dictionary. Spring-
  field, MA: G.&C. Merriman Company, 1965.

West, John Anthony. *The Traveler's Key to Ancient
  Egypt.* Wheaton, IL: Quest Books, 1995.

West, Shearer, ed. *The Bulfinch Guide to Art History.* Boston, New York, Toronto, London: A Bulfinch Press Book, Little, Brown and Company, 1996.

Weston, Richard. *Modernism.* London: Phaidon Press Limited, 1996.

Wharton, Edith, and Ogden Codman, Jr. *The Decoration of Houses.* New York: Classical America Edition, W.W. Norton & Company, 1997.

Whiton, Sherrill. *Interior Design and Decoration.* 4th ed. Philadelphia, New York, Toronto: J.B. Lippincott Company, 1974.

Wilhide, Elizabeth. *William Morris Decor and Design.* New York: Harry N. Abrams, Inc., 1991.

Wilkinson, Charles K. *Egyptian Wall Paintings.* The Metropolitan Museum of Art Bulletin, Spring 1979.

Wright, Frank Lloyd. *The Natural House.* New York: Plume Books, The New American Library, 1954.

Zerwick, Chloe. *A Short History of Glass.* The Corning Museum of Glass. New York: Harry N. Abrams, Inc., 1990.

Achromatic
Having no hue or color—as black, gray, or white—where in theory all colors of the spectrum are evenly absorbed or reflected.

Additive
The mixture of the colors of light. When all spectral colors are mixed the result is white light.

After-image
Also known as successive contrast, it occurs when the eye becomes fatigued by staring at a color. When focus is shifted, the color's complement is projected on the surface.

Aniline
A chemical derived from coal tar used in the creation of synthetic dyes.

Analogous
Generally, three adjacent colors on the artist's twelve-color wheel.

Apse
A recess, usually semicircular, which may have a coffered half-dome ceiling, at the east or altar end of a cathedral. The form was adapted from early Roman temples where recessed niches contained statues.

Arabesque
An interlaced pattern of spiraling or geometric forms or foliage used to decorate a vertical wall panel.

Baroque
A style in painting, sculpture, and architecture that began in Italy in the late sixteenth century and spread to France in the seventeenth century, as well as to other countries. As an artistic expression of free form and movement, baroque architecture is characterized by grand scale, exuberant curves, and a profusion of ornament.

Chiaroscuro
Derived from the Italian for "light" and "dark." The contrast of light and shadow in a painting to give it an illusion of depth and dimension.

Chinoiserie
A decorative motif based on the Chinese style, which was popular in eighteenth-century France and England.

Chroma
The intensity or saturation of a color.

Chromatic
A color that is highly saturated, or bright.

Cloisonné
A decorative item that is made of pieces of colored enamel held together by thin metal strips.

Cochineal
A parasitic insect which, like kermes, was a source of crimson dye.

Color constancy
The awareness that a color is basically constant, or the same color, under different lighting conditions.

Complement
The color directly opposite a color on the artist's color wheel.

Cornice
In interiors, a crown molding, or the projecting finishing piece that covers the seam between the wall and ceiling.

Cove
A concave recess in a wall that can run horizontally to connect the wall and ceiling, or vertically down a wall.

Dado
The lower part of a wall, treated in a different way from the upper portion. Usually wood, the dado is often paneled and has a base as well as a top cap to separate it from the upper wall.

Dye
A color that is soluble in the liquid in which it is mixed and that completely penetrates the material being colored.

GLOSSARY

Faux paint
The technique of painting on a wall, or other surface, to achieve texture or depth by glazing a color or value over another. It is also used to reproduce natural materials such as wood or marble.

Grisaille
Painting in different values of gray in order to make a surface appear three-dimensional or to simulate carved wood or marble sculpture.

Indigo
One of the earliest sources of plant dyes originating in Asia that produced a strong, dark, slightly grayed blue.

Kermes
A female insect that attached itself to the Mediterranean oak tree and was a source of crimson or scarlet dyes.

Lake
Animal or vegetable dyes which are added to a chalk-like powdered mineral to create insoluble pigments.

Luminance
The brightness or radiance of a color.

Madder
A plant whose roots were a major source of red dye in ancient and medieval times.

Metameric
Colors that match under one light source but not another are called a metameric match. For example, colors that match in daylight may not match under artificial light.

Millefleurs
French, meaning "thousand flowers." A fifteenth-century tapestry design showing a profusion of flowers and plants.

Mullion
A thin horizontal or vertical bar that separates glass panels.

Murex
A species of sea snail found in the Mediterranean, which produced a vivid purple dye. Because vast numbers were required to produce a minute quantity of dye, the color was reserved for the emperors of ancient Rome.

Neutral
Having no color; nearly achromatic.

Neutralized
In the case of a color, one that is grayed or whose brightness has been reduced to varying degrees by being mixed with its complementary color.

Ocher
A natural earth pigment, most often yellow or red in color.

Pastoral
A popular decorative theme in eighteenth-century France showing peasants or nobles in idyllic outdoor settings.

Paterae
An ornamental oval or round disk often decorated with a rosette.

Pigment
Finely ground powder which remains suspended and insoluble when combined with a binder, or vehicle, such as plant gum, egg, or the like. The binder becomes an adhesive to join the powder particles so they can be spread on a surface to harden.

Polychromy
Containing several or many colors—multicolored.

Primary color
A color that cannot be obtained by a mixture of other colors.

Refraction
The bending or breaking up of wavelengths of light as they pass from one medium to another, such as from air through glass.

Page 214: Detail, fresco of *Ladies in Blue*, Palace of Knossos (see p. 138).

Secondary color

A color that is obtained by the mixture of two primary colors.

Sfumato

Italian for "delicately shaded" or "smoky." Leonardo da Vinci used this technique of blurring the edges of objects in his paintings so they blended more softly into the background.

Shade

A color that is darkened through the use of black or a mixture of other colors.

Shagreen

Dried fish skin, often shark, which is used to cover furniture or decorative objects.

Sienna

A natural earth pigment that turns reddish brown when heated or "burnt."

Simultaneous contrast

The visual change in a color which occurs when it is placed next to another color.

Scagliola

An imitation marble made of colored gesso or plaster.

Spectrum

The electromagnetic spectrum is an energy field containing the visible spectrum of light and its wavelengths of color, as well as invisible rays such as radar, X-rays, and ultraviolet light.

Subtractive

The quality of having color taken away. In pigment mixing, the reduction of a color with another color which lessens its ability to reflect specific wavelengths of light. A mixture of all colors will subtract color, or reduce the mixture to brownish black.

Tertiary color

A color obtained by the mixture of a primary color with its adjacent secondary color.

Tint

A pale or very light color obtained by mixing a color with white.

Toile

A fabric showing pastoral scenes printed in one color on a white or cream background. The popular hand-blocked fabric was originally produced at Jouy, a town near Paris, in the eighteenth century.

Trompe l'oeil

French for "deceive the eye." A technique of painting that uses perspective, color, and/or shade and shadow to make objects or scenes appear three-dimensional. Examples are the painted scenes on the walls of Pompeii and Palladian villas that brought outdoor views into the interior.

Umber

A natural earth pigment that turns medium to dark brown when heated or "burnt."

Value

The lightness or darkness of a color.

Wainscot

Paneling on an interior wall, either partial or ceiling height. Panels can be large or small, framed by stiles (verticals) and rails (horizontal strips).

Woad

A plant whose leaves provided one of the earliest sources of blue dyes. Because of its abundance it was an inexpensive source of the color during the Middle Ages.

INDEX

PHOTOGRAPH CREDITS